WATCH THE **INTERVIEWS**

READ THE **BOOK**

WHICH WILL YOU DO FIRST? IT'S UP TO **YOU**

THE
OUTSIDER
INTERVIEWS

THE
OUTSIDER
INTERVIEWS

A New Generation
Speaks Out on Christianity

Jim Henderson, Todd Hunter, and Craig Spinks

BakerBooks

a division of Baker Publishing Group
Grand Rapids, Michigan

© 2010 by Jim Henderson, Todd Hunter, and Craig Spinks

Published by Baker Books
a division of Baker Publishing Group
P.O. Box 6287, Grand Rapids, MI 49516-6287
www.bakerbooks.com

Printed in the United States of America

ISBN 978-0-8010-1345-4

Photos of Jim Henderson and Craig Spinks appear courtesy of www.michaelwilsonphotographer.com.

Photos of Todd Hunter appear courtesy of www.tiffanyhixphotography.com.

10   11   12   13   14   15   16   7   6   5   4   3   2   1

For *the people Jesus misses most*

CONTENTS

WATCH THIS BOOK!

This is a DVD/Book—a DVB.

The DVD lets you see and hear people—their faces, gestures, and tone of voice. The book takes you behind the scenes to the authors' thoughts, dialogue, and disagreements. We placed the DVD inside the front of the book to send a message: you choose where to start.

It's up to you.

The book and DVD are different. Both contain compelling stories, thoughtful analysis, and practical ideas. Together they tell a story we hope will have an impact.

Think of it like seeing a movie with a few friends and then going out for coffee to talk about it. That is similar to what the three of us did. We facilitated the conversations, which you'll watch on the DVD, and then we went out and talked about what we learned, what surprised us, and so on, which you'll read about in the book.

You'll meet people you feel like you already know: friends, strangers, even your own kids. You'll meet some new people too.

Enjoy.

FOREWORD

I am excited about *The Outsider Interviews*.

As a survey researcher and a generational analyst, people often ask me where we actually find the people we interview. Our firm, the Barna Group, conducts telephone, online, and in-person interviews with tens of thousands of people every year. We employ sophisticated survey techniques and high-quality, nationwide samples. But if someone reads the data from our research and it does not fit their experiences, it is easy for them to wonder about the so-called science of survey research.

This happened frequently as a result of *unChristian*, the book Gabe Lyons and I collaborated on, which describes the next generation's growing disenchantment with Christianity. When the book was released, a lot of people had a hard time imagining that real people embraced such hostile—yet often very nuanced—views about the Christian faith. *Where did you find these people to interview? Why don't I know anyone like this? Do young people really perceive Christianity in such negative ways? None of the young people I know actually understand that much about the Christian faith. Don't young people just think whatever media tells them to think?*

I am enthusiastic about this book and DVD because I think this project begins to answer questions like these.

Actually, I understand why people are skeptical about research. There is no shortage of data available these days; most of it is not particularly good or reliable. And it is not easy to hear people critiquing the faith many of us follow.

Yet I think this resource from my friends Jim Henderson, Todd Hunter, and Craig Spinks is a fantastic way to get a "street-level" view of what young people think about the Christian faith. I have personally put in loads of hours trying to understand what Christianity looks like from an outsider's perspective. Yet this tool helped me remember the very human side of the thousands of interviews we have done. The video interviews put flesh and bones to the data—they made the stories come to life *because they involve real lives*.

Beyond the video segments with young people, I think you will be challenged by the conversations between Jim, Todd, and Craig recorded in the book. I participated in many of the live events during which the outsider interviews were filmed. I had a close-up look as Jim, Todd, and Craig worked their way from Phoenix to Seattle, Denver to Kansas City, trying to make sense of what they were learning. This book offers their observations filtered with a passion to help people see the real Jesus. I believe many of these conversations will stretch you as they did me.

Before letting you loose into reading the book or viewing the DVD (you choose where to start!), let me offer one last observation: isn't it ironic that one of the things that makes us human—our ability to hear and understand subtle inflections of complex sounds known as language—is also something we struggle with the most? Translation: for all our communication abilities, we don't listen very well. I suppose that makes some sense because our ability to communicate is deeply affected by our fallen natures. Just think about the common listening gaps: men versus women; wives against husbands; parents face off with children; employers agitate workers and vice versa; immigrants versus citizens; Christians against non-Christians. No matter what side of the fence you're on, we all struggle to understand others.

That was part of the reason I decided to use the terms "insiders" and "outsiders" in the book *unChristian*: they actually fit the way most of us think. For the most part we really do consider people "in" or "out," us versus them, Christians and everyone else. Don't get me wrong—I am more convinced than ever that we need to help people understand why they need Jesus. But this takes harder work than ever, and better, deeper reservoirs for hearing and perceiving the perspectives of those around us.

Ultimately this resource, like good research itself, should help us become better listeners. It will certainly make it harder to put people into neat little boxes.

Listen in on *The Outsider Interviews* with Jim, Todd, and Craig—three people I admire for their courage and transparency. They have let us in on their conversations and interactions with the next generation in hopes that all of us will grow into better people—more human, better listeners.

I am grateful to these three observers. And I hope they can help me find our next set of survey respondents!

David Kinnaman
Coauthor, *unChristian*
President, Barna Group

ACKNOWLEDGMENTS

Our editor, Chad Allen, is the person most responsible for this book seeing the light of day. He pursued us, put up with us, and pummeled us with questions that kept making the book better and better. He also stood up for us to the powers that be when we insisted that the book be combined with a DVD. He deserves a great deal of the credit for producing what we think of as the world's first DVB.

We are also grateful to the people who agreed to participate in this project. The Outsiders and Insiders who opened their hearts to us fearlessly voiced their opinions and helped us become more authentic followers of Jesus.

Special thanks goes to Kathy Escobar, Karl Wheeler, Beth Fitch, and Kirk Wulff. They are the people who spent some of their hard earned relational capital on this project by recruiting their Outsider friends to participate in these interviews. Thanks also go to Moutain View Lutheran Church in Phoenix, Christ Church Anglican in Overland Park, Kansas, Calvary Assembly in Seattle, The Refuge in Denver, and Alpha for providing venues and generous partnership.

It takes a village to write a book. Each one of our families has absorbed our attitudes, late night talks, and strange ideas ("What's a DVB?"). Consequently, special thanks goes out to Todd's wife, Debbie, and his children, Jonathon and Carol Hunter; Craig's wife, Sara, and his dad, Bob Spinks; and Jim's wife, Barbara, his three children, Joshua, Sarah, and Judah, and his first grandson, Huxley (aka "The Huckster") George Henderson.

Finally, it is with gratitude and humility that we acknowledge that *The Outsider Interviews* would have never transpired without the research and inspiration of David Kinnaman and Gabe Lyons's seminal work *unChristian*. We stand on their shoulders.

1

THE BACKSTORY

The Why, Where, Who, and How

Jim Henderson

> This chapter correlates with the video titled
> **"The Backstory"**
> on the Main Menu of your DVD.

No one likes to be called names, but that doesn't seem to stop us from coming up with new ones every day.

I lead Off The Map, an organization that helps Christians "see themselves through the eyes of outsiders." For the past ten years we've been researching the origins of the "us and them" mentality many Christians have and helping Christians bridge the insider-outsider divide. For some mysterious reason, evangelical Christians (my spiritual tribe) have devoted an unusual amount of energy toward developing a sophisticated linguistic system for identifying who's in and who's out.

What's more, as a result of our successful campaign to become America's civic religion, two interesting things have happened: "they" (outsiders) know we're here, and they have well-formed opinions about our habits and practices.

My first book was originally titled *A.K.A. Lost* because I wanted to take on the iconic status the word *lost* has gained in the Christian culture. Having been a pastor for twenty-five years, I had plenty of opportunities to observe how I and others used the word. After reflecting on my experiences, I came to the conclusion that for the most part, using *lost* as much as we did generally made us meaner people. It made it harder for us to connect with "lost" people. Frankly, it sounded like we were calling them a name. Perhaps what's most revealing is that we rarely use this word in the presence of actual lost people; we normally only use it *behind their backs*.

Cultures and social groups that create names to identify those who don't belong often become the most dangerous and meanest people on the planet. Think of racial slurs and the histories associated with them, for example. That's why we eventually came up with a new name to replace "lost": *the people Jesus misses most*.

When I read *unChristian* by David Kinnaman and Gabe Lyons, I discovered a word that I felt honestly described this divide.[1] I'm not saying I like this word, but it's certainly accurate. That word is *outsiders*. When we say *outsiders* out loud, particularly in the presence of people we label that way, we are held accountable. My contention is that if Christians want to create these divides, we at least should own up to them and say the word to outsiders' faces. Words are like mirrors; they reflect the images we hold in our minds back to us and confront us with them. In this book we will be holding this mirror up to Christians and asking them if they like what they see.

Blurring the Lines

What made *unChristian* even more important and provocative is that Kinnaman and Lyons not only queried outsiders but also asked *insiders* for their opinions about Christianity. The common denominator wasn't religion; it was age. Everyone they polled was between the ages of sixteen and twenty-nine. Focusing on this demographic allowed them to discover deep differences but also profound similarities.

Those experienced in sailing say that it is all about how you *angle into the wind*. By choosing to sail into this age group, Kinnaman and Lyons uncovered some surprising similarities between Christians and non-Christians, such as a high commitment to service, tolerance, and diversity, for example. They also uncovered this little-known fact: not only is there a divide between insiders and outsiders, but there is a divide between insiders and *insiders*. Thousands of young Christians are staying under the big tent of Christianity but refusing to toe the party line. They're resisting the more militant, doctrinaire, and strident elements of their host faith culture, particularly when identifying with these elements would marginalize those who don't hold the same views they do.

This is a significant shift. For example, when my generation (Boomers) discovered the inconsistencies of religion, we walked away from church, God, and Christianity. But this pragmatic, postmodern bunch is staying home and fighting for a new kind of Christianity. They're too committed to be pushed out of the house by those who think they're too soft on homosexuality, immigration, or abortion. They're on a mission to redefine what it means to be followers of Jesus in the real world and do it without becoming mean people.

After reflecting on the research, I was compelled to connect personally with some outsiders and insiders. I wanted to hear their voices and look them in the eye. I wanted to feel what it was like to call people outsiders to their faces and hear how they felt about our attempts to reach them, convert them, and (sadly) marginalize them. I wanted to let them know they were more than a number, more than a statistic or a demographic category. Besides calling them a name, I wanted to tell them that millions of other insiders and outsiders are struggling with the very same issues.

Three Amigos

Todd Hunter is one of the finest leaders I've ever worked with. He doesn't use leadership to work out his personal insecurities, and he actually develops people as leaders, not just as employees. But for the purposes of this project Todd brought one other important skill: curiosity. Todd likes outsiders and loves hearing their viewpoints. That's why I needed him on this team.

I hope you can keep this next bit a secret so I can continue relating to young people as well as I do for at least a few more years. Sometimes when I'm in a serious conversation with a twentysomething, I'm thinking to myself, *When is she going to realize I'm as old as her grandparents?* Anyway, Todd and I are honored to have a significant number of young leaders who relate to us. We both knew we needed one of these young leaders to be part of this project, so off we went to find Craig.

I met Craig Spinks when he was eighteen and I was fifty-one. That was almost ten years ago, when Craig was leading the video production team in the six-thousand-member church where we both worked at the time. Craig is a master storyteller with the video camera. He knows how to speak the visual vernacular, and at twenty-eight he falls inside the demographic Kinnaman and Lyons researched. Craig was raised in church and knows the insider stuff from a young person's point of view. I think you'll enjoy hearing his perspective throughout the book.

The People Jesus Misses Most

The three of us hit the road in the fall of 2008. We wanted to interview some outsiders and insiders in four different cities in America. Truth be told, we were just as interested in hearing from insiders, particularly about where they find points of agreement with outsiders. We also wanted to know what enabled them to call themselves Christians while still disagreeing with some of the main cultural ideas their spiritual elders fought so hard to establish over the past thirty-five years.

Even though we talked with both groups, we decided to call this *The Outsider Interviews* as a way of erring on the side of the people Jesus misses most. Dietrich Bonhoeffer said, "The church is the church only when it exists for others."[2]

We think the church has much to learn about connecting with outsiders. We have not sought them out for their opinions or asked them to help us become a better church. Instead we have often marginalized them and, worse, objectified them. We only need to look to our own lexicon for evidence of this trait. Here are a few of the names we've come up with to keep them in their place: *lost, unbelievers, unsaved, unrepentant, unregenerate, heathens*, and *reprobate*.

We wanted to change this bad habit. We wanted to let outsiders know we really do value their opinions and insights. We also wanted to model to the church the ancient practice of honoring the outsider. The Old Testament is filled with the stories of one famous outsider after another becoming central to the story of God—Tamar, Rahab, Ruth, Naaman, the entire city of Nineveh, and many Gentiles (like me), just to name a few.

As you will experience, this ancient approach continues to make an impression in the twenty-first century. More than one outsider told us they were shocked Christians were actually listening to them. Klarisa, an outsider in Kansas City, tore our hearts out when she said, "If Christians would listen and show some interest *in me*, I would be very open to their story." What if evangelism in our time is more about listening than speaking?

Cards on the Table

The three of us believe we're living in tumultuous times. For many young people, 9/11 is the controlling metaphor for the dramatic changes we find ourselves adjusting to every day. Financial markets are unpredictable, major world religions, including Christianity, are competing head-to-head for global market share, and it's commonly assumed that India and China will supersede the United States in terms of global influence (China is currently financing America's debt) sometime in the next fifty years.

The renowned strategic thinker Peter Drucker said, "Every few hundred years in Western society there occurs a sharp transformation. Within a few short decades, society rearranges itself."[3] The three of us are betting that we are currently living in that window of time and that some things, some big things, are never going back to the way they were. *Leave It to Beaver* has left the building. *Family Guy* has moved in, dirty laundry and all.

When Gutenberg introduced the printing press in the West, he had no idea what he was unleashing on the world. He was swinging a door on what Phyllis Tickle in *The Great Emergence* calls a "hinge time."[4] Many of us have never considered what the world must have felt like when Gutenberg was doing his thing. He was living in and helping to create a world caught between the times. Think about the experimentation, the uncertainty, the innovations, and the excitement that must have been taking place in such an environment. Fast-forward five hundred years and replace the printing press with the internet. Now think about this: the commercial use of the internet is only a little over fifteen years old. Most people in the world have yet to benefit from this incredible technology. Now think about the experimentation, uncertainty, and innovation that mark our time: MySpace, Facebook, Google, Twitter, the iPhone. How are followers of Jesus supposed to navigate these changes? How are we supposed to keep our spiritual equilibrium in a world caught between the times?

From Charts to Hearts

Being spiritual anthropologists we had to go see for ourselves if what Kinnaman and Lyons had to say was true. That's what motivated us to schlep our cameras, our support staff, and ourselves onto one plane after another. *We wanted to hear the stories behind the stats.* To use an exploration metaphor, we weren't satisfied with the view from the ship; we wanted to get in our canoes, row right up onto shore, beach our boats, and ask the natives what life looked like from their campfire.

A few years ago I had a speaking tour back east, so my wife, Barb, and I decided to drive between several of the events. Being members of AAA, we availed ourselves of their services and asked them to produce a detailed map of the routes from one city to another. They call this a TripTik. A TripTik is a very detailed and informative map. The only thing it does not provide is videos of where you're going. I can hear you saying, "But Jim, it isn't possible for a video to play inside a map, is it?" No, it isn't yet, though we're getting closer all the time. You get the idea. The reason we think a video map would be cool is because we are hardwired to want to *see* stuff. Just today I was watching yet another cooking show on TV with my wife. I asked her why she watched so many cooking shows. She said, "I like to see what they are doing; books don't provide enough of the details." Given the choice between words and pictures, most human beings, like my wife, will choose pictures.

UnChristian is like a TripTik for Christians. It provides information to help us navigate the road less traveled between ourselves and others. *UnChristian* provides the statistical information that explains how we got from where we were (the dominant religious voice in America) to where we are today (marginalized and mistrusted). What it doesn't show us is the faces behind these statistics. We can't see the people who are doing the talking. We can't see the hearts behind the charts.

Daniel Goleman, author of *Emotional Intelligence*, emphasizes the emotional power of the face. "Empathy depends on emotion and since emotion is conveyed nonverbally, *to enter another's heart, you must begin the journey by looking into the face.*"[5]

In this book you will see the faces and look into the eyes of outsiders.

Creating New Maps

We don't expect you to become spiritual anthropologists. However, because you are reading this book, we assume you like to travel to new places in your thinking. Our hope is that those who say they follow Jesus have an inclination to travel and see new things that expand their understanding of how he operates in the world.

The world Gutenberg inhabited over five hundred years ago is exactly the same earth you and I live on today. Same size, same continents—everything was as we find it today, more or less. Nevertheless, Gutenberg's world *felt much smaller than it actually was*. Here's why: the most popular maps in Gutenberg's time showed a world that dropped off the edge at the equator. Their maps showed a flat earth surrounded on all sides by giant waterfalls that spilled into the abyss. Consequently, almost every explorer stayed away from the edges and margins.

But Prince Henry was different.

Prince Henry the Navigator ruled Portugal fifty years before Columbus discovered America. He regularly dispatched mariners down the west coast of Africa until one returned and reported they had successfully crossed the equator and lived to talk about it.

When geopolitics change, we create new maps, like when the former USSR became a host of new countries ending in -*stan*. When boundaries change due to war, money, or negotiations, we create new maps, like when Rhodesia became Zimbabwe or Bombay became Mumbai.

The maps had to be redrawn. The world as they imagined it was turned upside down.

Just like in Prince Henry's time and ours, sometimes things happen that have never happened before. For example, here's a snapshot of what's been happening to the Southern Baptist Convention over the past seventy years:

1940–1960: enrollment in Sunday school grew from 3,590,038 to 7,382,550—an increase of over one hundred percent in twenty years

1960–2007: enrollment in Sunday school grew from 7,382,550 to 7,876,610—a 7 percent increase in forty-seven years

The Southern Baptist Convention isn't the only denomination in decline. Episcopalians are losing the equivalent of a diocese per year. Most if not all established denominations are going through a lot of upheaval these days.

We discovered in our interviews that a significant reshuffling is taking place in the socio-spiritual world in which Christianity is currently the dominant player. New players are emerging, new opportunities are opening up, and we need a new map.

Prince Henry's explorers proved the world people lived in was actually much larger than the one they *believed in*. Their discovery of *what had always been* laid the groundwork for new explorers and travelers. The funny thing is that the whole time they were arguing about the world being flat, they were doing it hanging upside down. The flat earthers were right about one thing: the lands around the equator *were* different—but these lands were not as dangerous as they'd been led to believe.

When it comes to understanding what outsiders think and feel, the church has inherited a map that is no longer accurate. Our map has too many equators and too few beaches. We need a map that properly represents the opportunities to meet new people and learn new languages. *We need a map that encourages us to travel to new places in our spiritual imaginations.* We need the kind of map the founder of our movement used to navigate his world.

Blaming Jesus

Let's face it: Jesus had several bad habits. Besides his penchant for claiming equality with God and his casual demonstrations of supernatural power, what *really* bugged his enemies was his habit of hanging out with sinners.

In fact, a simple reading of the Gospels reveals a clear fact: Jesus played favorites. He went easy on outsiders while raising the bar on insiders. He went out of his way to give sinners the benefit of the doubt but warned his followers to be careful around the religious.

Not only was Jesus liked and admired by outsiders, but he liked them back. We hear that Jesus loved people all the time, but our overuse of the word *love* can obscure things. A better word might be *like*. When I say I *like* someone, I'm basically saying I enjoy them, like their style, and respect their ideas. I am curious about what makes them tick and want to spend time with them. I'm relaxed with them, and they're relaxed with me.

What if we explained the gospel this way: *Jesus is the God who likes people!* I think most people would call that good news without us even telling them.

What We Hope For

I once heard Andy Groves, former CEO of Intel, say, "Leaders create experiences that move people to take action." In this project we've combined print and film to do exactly that. And what action do we want you to take?

Simply put, we hope *The Outsider Interviews* will inspire you to walk down to your local coffee shop and meet some of the people Jesus misses most. Notice them, pray for them (silently), and if one of them ends up trusting you, ask them this question, "How are you?"

Then put something in your mouth and listen.

KANSAS CITY OUTSIDERS

Christianity Has an Image Problem

Jim Henderson

This chapter correlates with the video titled
"Christianity Has an Image Problem"
in the Kansas City section of your DVD.

I've never had anybody say they want to save me and felt like
they truly loved me.

Klarisa

Whenever you and I get serious about change, psychotherapists, personal trainers, football coaches, piano teachers, and premarital counselors become our new best friends. They measure, probe, inspire, and even insult us. And we pay them to do it! A great example of this is the Body-for-LIFE weight loss program. Before you can begin, they require that you submit a *before* photo of you in your swimsuit for all to see. They know that seeing what you really look like in the mirror is the first step to real change.

But programs like Body-for-LIFE provide something else that's needed for real change to happen: a plan, a mental map that can lead us out of the past and into the future. Sometimes this map comes in the form of a person, sometimes it's a story, and sometimes it's three, seven, or twelve steps. Often, it's a combination of all three.

Our Outsider Interviews provide both experiences. On one hand, they're a mirror for Christians to see their reflection through the eyes of outsiders. On the other, they're a map to help insiders understand how to move forward and to connect with the people Jesus misses most.

In these interviews Craig, Todd, and I hold up quite a few mirrors, but the reality is that our first love is mapmaking. We want to inspire and enable Christians to travel to new places in their spiritual relationships. We want to provide Christians with an updated map of the cultural terrain as described by the people who are native to the area. For our purposes, those natives are often young people. Here's why.

If you've had the privilege of living in proximity to an immigrant community, you've likely noticed that the children often translate for the parents. That's because, as psychologist Ken Robinson once said at a conference I attended, "In immigrant communities *the children* go out and *teach their parents the culture*, the language, and the ideas." We think the same is true for Christians. When it comes to understanding the socio-spiritual terrain we now find ourselves living in, Christians over forty are the immigrants who ignore their children at their own peril. That's why both Kinnaman and Lyons and the three of us focused our attention on young people.

Christianity has an image problem. We can deny it, disdain it, and decry it, but the fact remains: in our culture the church is perceived as caring more about insiders than outsiders.

We've brought this on ourselves largely as a result of evangelicalism's successful campaign to become America's leading purveyor of religious goods and services. This means that even for Christians, *perception is reality*. And the way we're perceived, particularly by young people, is nothing short of alarming. Perhaps no one knows this better than David Kinnaman, president of the Barna Group and coauthor of *unChristian*—the book that originally sparked our interest in this project. In the same way Body-for-LIFE is both mirror and map, *unChristian* delivers both reality and hope.

First-person experiences of Christianity. Insiders and Outsiders tell it like it is.
Watch the clip
"Perceptions or Reality?"

In each Outsider Interview we highlight something we gleaned from *unChristian*. In this first interview we focused on what we see as the mother of all problems—the image problem. We wanted to learn how Christians come across to non-Christians and what we can do about it. And our guests were candid with us.

"These days nearly two out of every five young outsiders (38 percent) claim to have a 'bad impression of present-day Christianity.'"

Kinnaman and Lyons, *unChristian*, 24

We're Going to Kansas City

Situated near Kansas City in the leafy suburb of Overland Park, Christ Church Anglican is not what you'd call funky, but it is definitely a church committed to connecting with

outsiders. For several years they've used the Alpha program
to provide outsiders a place at the table, and when I say table,
I mean it quite literally. Alpha is an evangelism program
based on food, friendship, and authenticity. Each week small
groups of friendly Christians and curious outsiders meet for
dinner to discuss the meaning of Scripture and the doubts
of outsiders. Alpha is one of the few evangelism programs
based more on listening than talking.

The leader of the Alpha program at Christ Church is Kirk
Wullf. We asked Kirk to find the guests for this interview.
Amazingly, Kirk managed to get four people to agree to
sit on a stage with two strangers (Todd and me) and share
some of their deepest feelings about spirituality, religion,
and Christianity.

Kirk and I sat down just before the show to have an
interview of our own. I got things started by asking Kirk
how he managed to get this group of people to trust him.
He said, "I started hanging out at Starbucks for the first
two hours of my day while checking and writing email,
doing research for talks for classes that I would be teaching, and doing other work that didn't require me to be in
the office."

"Sounds to me like you treat connecting with people as if
it were a spiritual discipline."

"Exactly! At first I didn't *see* the opportunity, so like most
folks I would just dash in, grab my coffee, and be on my way.
But eventually what I found was a complete subculture that
I never knew existed. It was as if Starbucks was a modern
day 'water well,' the kind of place where Jesus might have
hung out. It didn't take me long, however, to discover that

this Starbucks was already a gathering place for people who already knew each other."

"Kind of like church?"

"Funny analogy, Jim, but yes, pretty close to the truth. Anyway, after hanging out there for a couple of months, I realized it was going to be difficult for me to 'break in' to that culture. I was the outsider! But a unique opportunity opened up. A new Starbucks was opening just a few blocks from our church. I kept watching for an opening date so that I could become a 'founding member' of this new Starbucks community, which is where I now put in most of my outsider hours."

"Is that where you found this great group?"

"Well, sort of. It's where I found Klarisa and where I found some other outsiders who helped me find some of the other people who eventually made it on stage with you."

"Sounds like there's more to this story than meets the eye."

"As always, Jim, as always . . ."

Craig was ready for us to get the show on the road. "Hey Jim, Jayson and I have a few last minute tweaks to make to the lighting, but why don't you and Todd bring the group on stage for the final sound check."

Jayson owns his own video business in Oregon. His job was to get the lighting and stage set up just right and run one of the three cameras that we used to shoot this interview. I often saw him only on stage because he'd fly in the afternoon of the show and out early the next morning.

We were finally mic'd up and ready to go. Craig counted us down.

Showtime

Most Christians have never seen an interview like this done in church. Of course we've all watched Oprah, Dr. Phil, and Leno do it, but for some reason we hardly ever think of using this format in church. That fact alone can create a sense of expectation, and Christ Church Anglican was buzzing.

"Please help me welcome our guests Tony, Sarah, Klarisa, and Dan."

I asked each guest to give us a little background and playfully added, "Who talked you into doing this interview anyway?"

Sarah is a flight attendant with Southwest Airlines. Her childhood religion, Roman Catholicism, didn't stick, but after coming to Alpha with her sister, she'd become a regular attendee at Christ Church. Ironically, she is still uncomfortable with the label "Christian" for some of the same reasons outsiders talk about.

Sarah and others describe their dilemma with the Christian brand.
Watch the clip
"The Christian Label."

Dan is also an ex-Catholic and now identifies himself as an atheist. He is a friend of a friend of Kirk who agreed to do the interview at the last minute as a favor to her. Tony is a special education teacher who came to faith. In spite of his determination to never become a Christian, Tony's friend in high school invited him to youth group, where he connected with Jesus in a serious way. The power of good people never ceases to amaze me. We're all suckers for love, kindness, and goodness. All it took was one good person, and Tony became a follower of Jesus.

Klarisa graduated from a university with a degree in nursing but soon decided that line of work wasn't for her and took a job at Kirk's Starbucks location. She had been born into a Jewish home. Her parents divorced and her mom remarried. Klarisa soon found herself being raised by a hyper-religious Christian stepfather (like Tony's) who also didn't do much to engender a love for the church in her. The quote that begins this chapter belongs to her.

Wanting to help our guests get comfortable, Todd tossed what interviewers call a softball.

"Do you guys agree with Kinnaman and Lyons that when it comes to Christians' image problem, swagger is our biggest issue?"

Tony jumped on Todd's pitch. "They think they're better than everybody else."

This wasn't coming from an outsider. Tony is a serious Christian who was talking about *his perception* of Christians. And that wasn't the worst of it. As the interview gained steam, we heard awful words to describe Christians. *Rude. Judgmental. Anti. Smug.*

> "The primary reason outsiders feel hostile toward Christians, and especially conservative Christians, is not because of any specific theological perspective. What they react negatively to is our 'swagger,' how we go about things and the sense of self-importance we project."
>
> Kinnaman and Lyons, *unChristian*, 26

And the statement about Christians that struck us as the most stinging of all: "They don't listen."

Our guests painted a vivid picture of what *swagger* looks like when it's dressed in religion. And unfortunately all of us insiders knew exactly what they were talking about.

As the Kansas City interview progressed, what I was picking up from the audience of about two hundred Christians, mostly over the age of fifty, was empathy, anger, and defensiveness.

I've been doing these types of interviews for ten years in front of thousands of Christians and have come to realize that while there are certainly exceptions, for the most part Christians are not accustomed to being talked down to, especially by non-Christians. In spite of the biblical injunction to humble ourselves under the mighty hand of God, knowing that in due time he will raise us up, we don't like to be insulted by non-Christians. We tend to cut them off, tell them where they have it wrong, and defend our practices, beliefs, and attitudes. In other words, "we don't listen."

I once read about a business that stopped hiring consultants and switched to *insultants*. As we listened to Klarisa explain how much she longed to have a Christian listen to her, I understood how we could benefit from that kind of shift. Outsiders not only hold up mirrors, they also show us a map—a way forward for those who might be interested in traveling to new places in their spiritual imaginations. If we "stay in the room" long enough, they eventually tell us how to go about fixing our image problem. We often close our interviews with this question: "If you thought Christians would listen to you, what would you tell them?"

Basically we were asking them to help us become better listeners. After some nervous glances to make sure we *really wanted to know* what they thought, our outsider and insider guests told us.

"Respect *my* views."

Klarisa was obviously deeply wounded and hypersensitive to the slightest hint of judgment. But she was also quite open to anyone who would take the time to understand and respect her views, which included her Jewish heritage.

"Make a friend."

Sarah works with gay people. She loves them. She told us we should make a friend without having an agenda. Just love them, she said.

Insiders and outsiders wonder if the Golden Rule still applies.
Watch the clip
"Is Love All You Need?"

"Be *for* something."

Tony is a Christian, just not the politically correct kind. He understood that for many people being a Christian meant being *against* abortion, against the Democratic Party, against stem cell research, against immigration, and against same-sex marriage. He wanted to know what they were *for*.

"Read the Bible."

Dan is an atheist who assumes that a fair reading of the Bible would solve the problem for most Christians. Dan believes the most important idea in the Bible is loving others the way you would like to be loved. He thinks that if Christians learned how to read Scripture accurately, they would see this and stop being judgmental.

Because Todd, Craig, and I live in different cities, these interviews are often the only time we get to see each other face-to-face. That's why we usually grab time immediately following each interview to compare notes and get our initial thoughts down on paper. But this time we all had prior commitments to keep, so our

> "One outsider put it this way: 'Most people I meet assume that *Christian* means very conservative, entrenched in their thinking, antigay, antichoice, angry, violent, illogical, empire builders; they want to convert everyone, and they generally cannot live peacefully with anyone who doesn't believe what they believe.'"
>
> Kinnaman and Lyons, *unChristian*, 26

writers' recap meeting would have to take place over the phone.

As soon as the show was over, Todd turned to me and said, "Jim, I'm really sorry, but I have to get right to the airport. I have a cab waiting. Can the three of us get on the phone sometime next week?"

"Sure, Todd. Where are you headed?"

"You know how I told you that I've been in discussions with the Anglicans about starting a church planting network on the West Coast?"

"Yeah, something about two hundred churches in twenty years?"

"Right. Well, they're really getting serious about this, and now they want me to become a priest."

"You, a priest, Todd?" I was surprised. Todd had become a Christian during the Jesus People era and gotten involved with the Vineyard movement, but he'd been part of nothing close to Anglicanism that I had heard of.

Craig overheard the words *priest* and *Todd* in the same sentence and dropped the cables he was packing up.

"Did I hear you say something about becoming a priest, Todd? Does your wife know about this?"

I was enjoying the moment.

"Look, you guys leave me alone," said Todd. "Anyway, Anglican priests get to be married, so Debbie is cool with the whole thing. I have to catch a cab. Like I said, let's continue this harassment over the phone next week."

And with that, Todd, who flies so much that he confuses the executive lounge with his home office, was off for yet another airport.

When we were planning this DVB, Craig suggested that he shoot an in-depth interview with each guest after the show. This would give him time to dig into some of the more personal issues and provide interesting comments. He was getting ready for that segment, so I knew he wouldn't be available to compare notes with me either.

I thanked all our guests, paid the house band, said my good-byes to the production team, and headed for my hotel. I had a super early morning flight to catch, and I still needed to outline the story that was emerging out of this Outsiders Interview.

Just as I was beginning to think about sleep, the phone rang. It was Craig.

"Jim, you still up?" Craig was obviously *not* thinking about sleep. He was pretty excited and wired from shooting four hours of one-on-one interviews with our guests.

"Uh huh," I mumbled into the phone.

"Hey, Jayson and I want to grab a bite to eat; we found a cool section of Kansas City we want to check out. Meet us in the lobby in fifteen minutes."

"Hey, Craig? You there, Craig?"

Craig had hung up. He wasn't interested in hearing I had to get up at 4:30 a.m. to catch a flight.

Because I'm really a blues musician trapped in the body of a pastor, I had some inner resources to draw on. When I worked in bands, I would often play till 1:00 a.m. and then head to some twenty-four-hour restaurant to hang out with the guys I just gigged with.

Craig and Jayson showed up in a rental car, and I piled into the back. We ended up in one of the loudest restaurants I've ever been in. It was impossible to talk, so I played the old guy card and asked if we could find another place. We pushed our way through the crowd of young people stacked three deep in every direction. We found a quiet bar where I could finally hear Craig's voice.

"Jim, you would have loved my interview with Klarisa. She shared a powerful story that shed a little more light on her sensitivity toward being judged."

"Oh, good. She seemed really sensitive about that issue."

"Well, a while back, following a very short-term relationship, Klarisa discovered she was pregnant. Finding herself in a moral dilemma, she asked some friends whether or not she should get an abortion. Interestingly, the friends she chose to talk with about this were Christians. As you might guess, her Christian friends told her getting an abortion was out of the question. This troubled Klarisa because for her the decision was not as clear-cut, and she felt as though her friends were willing to put their friendship on the line if she chose to get an abortion. However, one friend was different. This friend, also a Christian,

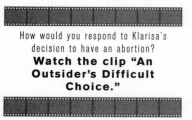

How would you respond to Klarisa's decision to have an abortion?
Watch the clip "An Outsider's Difficult Choice."

shared that she didn't think abortion was the best option but also recognized the complexity of Klarisa's decision. She said she would be there for Klarisa no matter what she chose. Klarisa ended up deciding to have an abortion, and her friend stayed true to her word; she even took Klarisa to the clinic. Jim, this story is so powerful to me because Klarisa's friend decided to set aside her own feelings and be there for Klarisa in a time when others wouldn't. Klarisa even went as far as to say that this friend is the *only* reason she can still see Christianity in a positive light."

Jayson, who's from Oregon, the state where people who identify themselves as having no religion comprise the fastest-growing faith segment, finished his beer and decided to play devil's advocate. "So, Craig, are you saying it's okay to get an abortion and that Christians should just go with the flow?"

"I'm not saying what's right and wrong. What I am saying is that Klarisa's experience is real and for better or worse is common in our world. I was amazed that her Christian friend had the capacity to support her even when she made a choice her friend didn't approve of. While I'm sorry about the loss of life, I'm hopeful that Klarisa's friend's sacrifice to stay connected has had a powerful impact on Klarisa."

"But aren't you guys afraid that Klarisa will see her friend's actions as approval?"

"Not a chance, Jayson. Klarisa understood that ultimately her Christian friend did not approve of her choice even though she offered emotional support. Klarisa also knew this friend was the only person who was willing to accompany her to the abortion clinic. This dilemma sounds similar to some of the stuff I read about Jesus in the Bible. It must have been those kinds of situations that got Jesus in hot water with the religionists of his day."

Jayson countered with, "But Klarisa also said that her friend said to her afterward that 'it was the best of the options.' You don't see that as support?"

"Actually, Jayson, I *do* see that as support—support for Klarisa as a person. At that point Klarisa's friend could have said 'I told you so,' but instead she chose to say, 'I see that you're going through a rough time. I know you considered your options carefully and made the choice you thought was best. Hang in there.' I don't think Klarisa confuses her friend's support as approval for abortion. Remember, Klarisa introduced her friend as being 'very much pro-life.'"

I interrupted, "Hey guys, I really need to get a few hours sleep. I have a 6:00 a.m. plane to catch."

Craig pulled the rental into the circular driveway of the hotel. It was 1:30 in the morning, a time when even cool people like me get tired when they're sixty-one.

"Jim, make sure to set up that conference call with Todd in the next few days so we get something on paper. Oh, and good luck getting some rest!" With that the two young hipsters headed out for another beer and more conversation.

On the flight home I wrote an email to Todd and Craig. "Hey guys, let's set up our first call for next Thursday at 10:00 a.m. Pacific. Let me know if this works for you."

Like a lot of other people, we have had our lives changed by email. We live in three different cities—Craig in Denver, Todd in Boise, and me in Seattle—yet we can work online and over the phone as if we were in the same office. I don't know about others, but I feel as if I was born for such a time as this.

Nevertheless, I hate conference calls. They're impersonal. I like watching people's eyes when they talk. That's how I get what they're really saying. I especially dislike speakerphones. They are so Donald Trump. But I connected my speakerphone and dialed in to the call.

I was the first one on the call, but not for long.

"Todd here."

"Hey Todd, how's the weather in Boise?"

"Craig here."

"Weather's really nice, Jim. Hey Craig, what's up?"

Technology really forces you into simultaneous conversations. The younger the natives, the more natural this form of communication is.

"So Todd, are you a priest yet?" Craig was picking up where he left off in Kansas City.

"Next week, Craig. I head over to Costa Mesa where my new church plant will be. That's where they want to do the ordination ceremony."

I jumped in. "What's the name of the church you're planting, Todd?"

"Holy Trinity Anglican Church."

"That sounds incredibly holy!" Craig wasn't going to let up on Father Todd.

The three of us are like brothers. We tease in ways others can't. But we also have each other's back.

I yelled into the speakerphone, "Hey guys, let's get something on paper. Craig, you're the one tasked with finding the main story in each interview. How about Kansas City? What's the big picture?"

"Simple, Jim. The church has an image problem, specifically with something outsiders call 'swagger.'"

Todd was already talking over Craig. "Hey, can you guys hear me?"

Craig surrendered telephonic control.

"Craig, it's just like Jim said earlier: *unChristian* is the mirror and *swagger is the image* we see staring us back in the face. Not a pretty picture but not an entirely bleak one either. Just a few years ago, if people were asked to list the ten biggest problems the church faces, 'the swagger of Christians' would have not have made the list. 'Church is boring,' 'the music is bad,' 'the preacher is irrelevant' would have.

43

I don't mean to sound simple, but I think all we need is to offer outsiders a good apology."

The clatter of Craig's typing in the background went silent. His voice was strained—slightly tense, the way we sound when we're nervous. My wife calls it the high voice.

"Apology, Todd? That sounds suspiciously close to *apologetics*. Is that what you mean?"

Not being a big fan of the whole business of apologetics either, I imagined the phone was a TV and stared, waiting to see how Todd would answer Craig's question.

"What are those three favorite words of yours, Jim? *Hear, listen, connect*? That's what I mean by a good apology, which in this case also happens to serve as an apologetic."

Craig was ready to jump on Todd.

"How so, Dr. Hunter? In my experience apologetics has come to mean to argue, defend, or even belittle. How do apologize and apologetics go together?"

The phone went quiet. Todd paused and then spoke.

"Craig, when I said a couple of minutes ago that the news in Kinnaman's mirror wasn't entirely bleak, here's what I meant. If *unChristian* teaches us anything, it's this: spiritual transformation for the sake of others is a new apologetic. Outsiders are telling us that they can't trust us as conversation partners because of our swagger. It's not our doctrine but our manner of being that stops the conversation. But a follower of Jesus who, as Jim says, *hears, listens*, and *connects* opens that conversation back up. In that sense we become a walking, living, breathing apologetic. That's what I mean by a new apologetic. Does that resonate?"

Craig's voice was back to normal. "Yeah, that makes more sense, Todd. Sorry for the pushback. I'm just a little gun-shy when religious language starts getting tossed around. But you can count me in as being a human apologetic."

Todd wasn't done.

"Just for the record, Craig, I think outsiders are being used by God as prophets! From Moses to Jesus to Paul, our sacred text is really high on humility and love and really down on the things outsiders are down on. We Christians can change. We can take on new attitudes of the heart and the words and deeds that flow from a transformed heart."

Beep-beep-beep-beep. . . . Technology had once again cut off a sacred moment.

I dialed back in, and soon the three of us were back at it.

"You guys there?" I yelled into the weird, boomerang-shaped speakerphone.

Craig was first. "I'm here, Jim."

"Me too, but I've only got a few more minutes, Jim. More meetings, more conference calls." Priests are busy people.

I had one more item on my list that I wanted to process with Todd and Craig, something I call the Christian consultant phenomenon. I knew the clock was ticking, so I jumped in.

"Todd, your comment about Christians being able to change—to do the right thing—made me think of something. Did you guys notice that all four of our guests have a close friendship with at least one Christian? I call these people Christian consultants. Tony and Sarah both came to faith in spite of their negative experiences with other Christians because of that person. It shows that perceptions can be changed fairly quickly by one person."

"Jim, can you guys hear me?" Todd was excited.

"Go for it, Todd."

"Hey, your comment about one person shifting perceptions reminded me of an interaction I had recently at a car rental company. I had just landed in Houston when it hit me that I had forgotten to reserve a rental car. As soon as we got the green light to use our cell phones, I got on the phone with a rental company. I needed to get a car right away because I had to speak at a major fundraiser that night. So someone named Sally gets on the phone and says the normal 'How may I help you?' I explained my situation and gave her my member number. She asked if I could hold, which as you know often means, 'I don't want to tell you no, so I hope after waiting ten minutes on hold you will hang up and not call back.' Amazingly, Sally did get back to me in about thirty seconds with 'Mr. Hunter, would you like that car in red or black?' I told her black, and she said the car would be waiting for me when I got off the shuttle and there was no need for me to come inside since she had already handled all the paperwork. My point is that I will never forget Sally or her company. It's always about one person. Human beings relate to each other, not to organizations, companies, or even religions."

We could hear Craig multitasking, but Todd's comment about how we relate to people, not organizations, compelled him back into the conference call.

"That's what surprised me about Klarisa and Dan as well. Both of them got to our stage largely due to the influence of a couple of Christians they respect and trust. We absolutely need to communicate the power of this idea to our readers and viewers. It is very hopeful."

"Hang on, you guys, Vivian needs something." While Todd's assistant, Vivian, had his attention, Craig and I kept the conversation going.

"Craig, tell me more about what you just said."

"What's that, Jim?"

"Something about needing to communicate the power of this idea to our readers and viewers. What idea are you talking about?"

"The idea that listening is more than just a means to an end."

Craig had talked to me about this issue before. I could hear the passion in his voice as he continued. "It seems to me that respectful listening is somewhat of an afterthought for much of the church and in some cases is even used as a manipulative tool for getting others to listen to us. I'd love for people reading this book to start thinking of listening as a spiritual discipline. Like Kirk uses Starbucks—he's not going there to evangelize but to talk with people. He counts being with people as a sort of discipline, what you call 'otherlyness,' Jim. It's the power of one person paying attention and being curious about another person's life. But our listening can't stop there. It can't become an 'I'll scratch your back if you scratch mine' kind of thing. Klarisa's friends probably listened to her, but when she said the wrong thing and opened up about considering abortion, they stopped listening and started preaching. Listening doesn't mean we can't share our own views. Listening means we're respectful and kind no matter how much we disagree."

"Do you guys remember," I responded, "the moment during the interview when I turned to Klarisa and said, 'So Klarisa, what you're saying is, in spite of all the negative experiences you've had with Christians, if a Christian did listen, was curious, and did show respect for your current beliefs, you would be happy to hear what they had to say?'"

Insiders and outsiders agree: we need to talk less and listen more. **Watch the clip "I Need Someone to Listen."**

"I do remember that," Craig said. "She was beaming, very authentic. But the words Klarisa spoke earlier are what really haunt me."

"What was that, Craig?"

"She said, 'I've never had anybody say they want to save me and felt like they truly loved me.' I can't get that out of my mind."

3

THINGS CHANGE

Billy Graham's Socks and the Threat of Postmodernity

Todd Hunter

Let's practice what we've been preaching and start this chapter by listening to some of the things our guests in Kansas City told us. Here's what I heard:

"We like Jesus's teachings . . . but Christians don't follow them."

Klarisa didn't just want Christian ideas *told* to her, she wanted Christianity *explained* to her in a *conversation*—one where she got to talk as well.

Outsiders believe the only things Christians care about is being right and proving others wrong. They believe that in conversations with Christians there is an undercurrent of arrogance.[1]

They say they object not so much to our belief system as to what they call our *swagger*.[2]

It's stunning to see the words *arrogance* and *swagger* attached to followers of Jesus, isn't it? It would be one thing if these criticisms were at-a-distance stereotypes, but unfortunately these observations come from real-life, up-close encounters with Christians.

While I am very sure *swagger* is not true of all Christians, it's true enough that it is now assumed by the majority of young outsiders.[3]

The research from *unChristian* shows that:

- outsiders express their highest levels of opposition toward *evangelical* Christians,[4] and
- like a corrupted computer file or a bad photocopy, Christianity, they say, is no longer in pure form. One quarter of outsiders say that their foremost perception of Christianity is that *the faith has changed for the worse.*[5]

By the way, before we go too far here, did you catch the epigraph at the beginning of the previous chapter? *"I've never had anybody say they want to save me and felt like they truly loved me."* This sentiment captures some of what has changed over the past few decades. That's because *answers* and *decisions* as the first instincts of seekers have given way to *relationship* and *acceptance.* That's what Klarisa and the other outsiders were asking for in Kansas City—relationship.

All models and methods of evangelism spring forth from an era, a social condition. When Billy Graham was at the height of his success, there was, in comparison to today, a low level of resentment between insiders and outsiders. Can you recall someone saying, "I watched a Billy Graham

Crusade on television (or went to a stadium to hear him) and thought he was a flake"?

Arguments were employed more easily when people basically agreed with the main principles of the faith and were just looking for a nudge to make a decision. Read the words in the next paragraph. I'll bet you can not only call to mind the right picture but also, unless you are a really young reader, hear Billy's utterly unique tone of voice. Picture and hear Billy giving an invitation:

"You may have gone to church when you were young . . . you may have been baptized . . . you may have been confirmed . . . but tonight you know you do not have a personal relationship with Jesus Christ . . . and so I'm going to ask you to come . . . to make a decision . . ."

I am not criticizing Billy Graham—you'll see where I am going in a moment. In fact, I am such a fan of Billy Graham that good friends of mine have often teased me that if I ever got fired from my job, I'd probably end up as the curator of the Graham Museum. But did you catch that last word? *Museum.* Graham has a museum dedicated to his life's work. Actually he has two: one at Wheaton College in Illinois and one in Charlotte, North Carolina. Billy is so famous, so admired and respected, that he has surpassed even being a brand. For him personhood has turned into institution.[6]

But as great a person as Billy is—and he is a person of enormous character, gifts, ability, and integrity—he was not always an institution. He is so respected today that people have forgotten Billy Graham was a controversial risk taker as a young evangelist.

Graham, reflecting on his early years, said, "We used every modern means to catch the attention of the unconverted."[7]

What were some of these attention-seeking methods? Graham and his team were well known to wear "garish, neon glo-sox," argyle socks, and hand-painted ties;[8] they wore "bright suits that all the world might know Christianity to be no dreary faith."[9] And Cliff Barrows was known to be on stage with a trombone or even a "consecrated" saxophone.[10]

What in the world is a *consecrated* sax—and why would anyone care? Why were loud clothes or a trombone of any consequence? Here's why. In the 1940s they were all symbols of the evil of the big band music of the Roaring Twenties. It would have been something like being heavily pierced and tattooed a few years ago—not cool to parents and not cool to the Youth for Christ board of directors who had just hired this young Mr. Graham.

I sometimes have wondered if someone on the YFC board ever thought of firing Graham and his team for their "excesses" of attire. Just think, you might have never heard of Billy Graham—and history would have been different.

In other words, Billy did his amazing work in a setting that is different from ours. Billy spoke to crowds of people who at least knew the felt board versions of Zacchaeus up the tree, Jesus driving out the money changers, Jonah and the fish, and so on. That is not the case today. We can no longer assume that when most people come to faith, they are making personal something that was already familiar to them.

A number of years ago I was told by a professor of evangelism that the average person who came down to the field in a stadium to receive Christ had experienced four positive contacts with Christians or the church. About fifteen years later, another professor said that the number had grown to sixteen positive contacts before a person responded. Today, research from David Kinnaman shows that mass evangelism can often cause more negativity than positive reaction.[11]

How do we explain this? Simple: *things change.*

Cultural climates have changed in every which way over two thousand years of church history. But God has never been checkmated or rendered unable to respond lovingly. We do not need to get bogged down in a lot of history or theology. We just need to remember this: *there is no such thing as effective evangelism that is not reflective of its cultural context.*

Graham's form—and he is the archetype of many others—did not come out of the blue. It arose precisely within a context, a context that held power for most of the history of America and especially in the decades following World War II. This context was marked by modern ways of thinking and a Christendom vibe. But things started to change in the 1960s and picked up steam with the cynicism following Vietnam and Watergate. Modern ways of handling truth, religion, and church have been in turmoil for the past twenty years.

"Anchored to the Rock . . . Geared to the Times"

"Anchored to the Rock . . . Geared to the Times." Those two phrases comprised the slogan of Youth for Christ when Graham began doing evangelistic meetings with them. Whatever Billy did to try to relate to the inquirers at his events, he did to stay both geared to his times and anchored to the rock of the biblical story.[12] Though Billy was the finest example of this in our lifetime, he was not the first. The Bible tells us two stories about how necessary and difficult this process of being anchored and geared can be.

The first story is that of Peter and Cornelius (see Acts 10). If you are like me, you probably think of the story as "the conversion of Cornelius and his household." I read the story that way as well until about ten years ago when I heard my friend Brian McLaren expound on the text and show how Peter had to be "converted" before he could be used by God to bring God's grace, forgiveness, and new life to Cornelius's household. I instantly saw Brian's point and wondered why I'd never seen it before!

Think about it: Jews were not to have close fellowship with gentiles. Thus being faithfully Jewish meant not doing what the vision was asking Peter to do. God had to repeat it and get a little forceful with Peter before Peter was willing to see Cornelius as "clean" and go to his house.

Paul tried to walk a similar line. Giving us a glimpse into his inner world, he said:

> I have voluntarily become a servant to any and all in order to reach a wide range of people: religious, nonreligious, meticulous moralists, loose-living immoralists, the defeated, the demoralized—whoever. I didn't take on their way of life. I kept my bearings in Christ—but I entered their world and tried to experience things from their point of view. I've become just about every sort of servant there is in my attempts to lead those I meet into a God-saved life. I did all this because of the Message. I didn't just want to talk about it; I wanted to be in on it!
>
> 1 Corinthians 9:19–23

Paul didn't use the anchored/geared language, but you can hear his heart: "I entered their world . . . I tried to experience things from their point of view . . . but I did not lose my bearings in Christ . . . I didn't take on their way of life . . ."

Quite the tap dance, huh? Connecting with outsiders can be scary, pushing us out of our comfort zone. The reality is that *there is no risk-free way of doing evangelism,* of simultaneously staying anchored to the rock and geared to the times.

If we are to do as Paul, Peter, and Billy Graham have modeled for us, we must first ask the question, "What is different about *our* time, and how do we remain relevant?"

Billy came on the scene when the modern worldview went unchallenged in mainstream society. Christianity was largely respected. It certainly was not being bashed in the media. With that in mind, we can say that a partnership between the modern world and Christianity gave rise to Graham. Remember, there is no such thing as models of evangelism which are disconnected from their culture.

> ### unChristian Research
>
> The three of us have been deeply impacted by the research emerging from *unChristian.* I'm on record as having said in many cities that I think it is one of the most important evangelism and ministry books of the last decade. The facts are not for the faint of heart, and coming to terms with the implications will take courage, but we have no other option than to listen. We are the ones who are alive now. We have to deal with it—even if it scares us—for there is no risk-free way to engage the culture in a conversation about faith.

We could just as accurately say that a partnership between the ancient Roman world and Christianity gave rise to the rapid growth of Christianity in its early years. Roads that enabled travel, the cultural acceptance of free-flowing ideas (as long you paid homage to Caesar), and forums for public discourse were what made the early missionary journeys possible.

What about us? What about the early part of the twenty-first century?

The New Atheism

"What's new," you might ask, "about something as old as atheism?" The current brand is not your normal, humble, I'm-not-convinced-about-God atheism. It is down on religion and the church to a whole new degree. A succession of bestselling books have torn into religion:

- *The End of Faith* by Sam Harris
- *The God Delusion* by Richard Dawkins
- *God Is Not Great: How Religion Poisons Everything* by Christopher Hitchens

These new atheists

- condemn not just belief in God but also respect for belief in God;[13]
- say religion is not just wrong, it is evil; thus atheistic evangelism is a moral imperative;
- assert that atheism is virtuous—as righteous and honorable as those who worked against slavery;
- seek to deliver our children from God-based falsehoods—as previous generations did when fighting against slavery or the belief that the earth was flat;
- argue that bad ideas foisted on children are moral wrongs;

- think that unless we renounce faith, religious violence will soon bring civilization to an end.

An article in *The Economist* summed up the atheistic viewpoint well: "When historians look back at this century, they will probably see religion as 'the prime animating and destructive force in human affairs.'"[14]

I think you might agree with me that when the question changes from "Is the church cool?" to "Is the church evil?" we have a larger problem on our hands. It is one thing for "cool" to lurk beneath *swagger, but quite another for evil to do so.*

Postmodernism

The contemporary world is rife with skepticism regarding the modern, scientific, empirical worldview that was handed down to us over hundreds of years of history. Why? Such views do not seem experientially true. People—especially young people—are tired of being spun, sold, lied to, and manipulated. So much so, in fact, that they wonder what is *not* spin or hype or when something is being forced on them.

This is not to say that proclamation or propositions or "facts" are no longer valid. It is to say that people access, hold on to, and pass on truth in a variety of ways. It is to say that in our present time relationships, community, and conversation are prized over empiricism and rationalism— even though people actually live their lives in very rational ways.

Frankly, I don't think we actually live in the postmodern world. I think we live in something even more unsettling—we live in a time between the times. A new world seems to be coming down the birth canal while the other one is not yet in the grave. As my friend Len Sweet has said, most young people today are natives to this new culture. But we *older* folks are strangers in a strange land—and we feel it. We feel much the way Peter and Paul must have felt. We're trying to figure out a whole new reality.

Post-Christendom

The "post" in post-Christendom points to something after Christendom. *Christendom* is a socio-historical term referring to times and places where the church has been granted status in culture. This status was first given by governments or royalty but can also be granted by pop culture, such as Billy Graham's acceptance as "America's pastor."

Christendom refers to the time when the old white steeple on the corner of 1st and Main in most small cities in America did not just dominate the architecture of the corner on which it sat but likely dominated the psychology of the town.

My little town of Eagle, Idaho, is an example of this. Three churches once sat within a block or two of our "1st and Main." These three churches did dominate the culture of Eagle. Now? Now one of those churches is a coffee shop, one is a furniture store, and the other a secondhand shop. I'm not arguing that it is wrong to renovate churches. I'm simply pointing out that the past religious reality of my little town, and many others, is now gone, replaced by commerce.

Most of us over the age of thirty can remember when the church and Christianity were respected as players at the tables of power in society. To have this status suddenly taken away and on top of that to be told that *we're the problem* is a difficult pill to swallow.

Klarisa's Clarion Call to Conversation

For Jim, Craig, and me, the number one takeaway from our experience in Kansas City was the confirmation of our thesis: the church can no longer proclaim from a distance and do well with young outsiders. Like Peter, we've got to risk getting in their "homes." Some have referred to this practice as that of "presence"—we must *be with* those around us. Our personal, even physical, presence matters.

Closely connected to presence is the persuasive evangelistic power of listening. Check that: *the persuasive evangelistic power of listening*. We need to pay attention to this for two reasons.

First, virtually every young outsider I meet has some negative, firsthand story to tell about Christians. My anecdotal research is supported by the more careful science behind *unChristian*.[15] We need to let them tell these stories and listen without judgment. But don't worry: conversation means, by definition, two-way communication. If you'll let them tell their story, at some point they will usually stop and say something like, "So what do you think?" Then it is time for you to talk, to comfort, to tell your story of redemption, and so on.

Second, when we had a modern world that loved and valued experts, it gave rise to a kind of evangelism in which churches' experts could stand on high stages and talk to masses of people. But in the midst of postmodernism and post-Christendom, the culture is calling for conversation, dialogue, and sitting on the same level.

This listening bit can be challenging; some fear "conversation" sounds too much like "compromise." But as Paul suggests in the passage above, we must learn the power of entering another's world.

Have you ever caught an episode of *The Tonight Show with Jay Leno* in which he was doing his "Jaywalking" segment with his microphone in hand, asking questions out on Hollywood Boulevard? Imagine Jay decides to play word association. Putting his microphone to the mouths of people on the street, he says, "Evangelicals." How many people do you think Jay would have to interview before he heard the words "really good listeners"?

Let's keep this real. We simply don't have a reputation for listening. But if our guests in Kansas City are in any way reflective of others, we need to get comfortable being uncomfortable. We need to become experts at being in conversations we don't control.

In times past we rightly assumed that people mostly listened their way into faith. That meant we played the role of the *talker*. Today seekers often *talk* their way into faith. They tell their stories, ask their questions, make observations, and so on. That places us in the role of *hearing*, *listening*, and *connecting*. This, by the way, is why Alpha courses like the one at Christ Church work so well. When people's deepest questions and concerns are listened to in the context of Christian hospitality offered through a nice meal, friendship, teaching, and a conversation that follows, you have the ancient and future formula for effective evangelism.

Evangelism Has Gone Spiritual

Hearing, listening, and connecting must be authentic qualities of being. They cannot merely be tactics. Most everyone in our culture is both used to and sick of being sold things. They know instinctively when someone is being nice just to sell them a product or service. If hearing, listening, and connecting are mere tactics, if they are not rooted in genuine, altruistic love, they become deceitful forms of manipulation.

In other words, surprisingly, evangelism is moving away from programs and mass systems and is *going spiritual*. It is going in the direction of spiritual formation. Kinnaman and Lyons call a lack of authentic spiritual formation *unChristian* lives. I am talking about the same thing here when I talk about *unformed* lives. Kinnaman said these unChristian lives were a major barrier to outsiders coming to faith.

Spiritual formation is now a huge doorway to faith. *Today's outsiders are looking first for what's real, not what's right*. Later they will ask "What's right?" or "What should I believe?" Listening and engaging their lives with genuineness opens doors and widens eyes, and it creates the kind of conversation in which the gospel can be openly discussed.

God Is Not Stumped!

Here's some good news: God is not stumped by the current state of affairs. He is not anxiously pacing the golden streets, saying, "Oh, myself! What am I going to do? I did not anticipate postmodernism! Quick, Peter, do a Google search: what in my home's name are epistemology and deconstruction? Who are Foucault, Derrida, and Rorty?"

Do you think God's will is actually in jeopardy because of a few philosophers? Do you see this as a chess game in which God is trapped?

I certainly don't!

Here's what I think. Somewhere out there is a twenty-something man or woman (or group of men and women) who is the next Billy Graham. (Not in the way Billy was, because as stated earlier, all approaches to evangelism are contextual.)

The God *who is not stumped* is raising up young people, natives to this culture, who will create new models that practice *hearing*, *listening*, and *connecting*.

4

PHOENIX OUTSIDERS

Beliefs and Blinders

Jim Henderson

This chapter correlates with the video titled
"Beliefs and Blinders"
in the Phoenix section of your DVD.

Todd Hunter hosts several "Conversational Evangelism Conferences" each year and often asks Off The Map to produce them. Todd's conferences include a virtual who's who of evangelism. Speakers like Becky Pippert, Lee Strobel, Mark Mittelberg, Elisa Morgan, Dan Kimball, Rick Richardson, Garry Poole, Randy Siever, David Kinnaman, and Dick Peace join Todd for a couple of days to unpack the best practices in evangelism. Behind the scenes the team and I get to hang out with these leaders, which is a real treat. As the executive producer I get to see how famous people respond when I start "bossing" them around. I feel like a basketball coach trying to get all these gifted players their minutes. It's a delightful challenge.

Speaking of bosses, I was getting ready for the pre-show dinner in Phoenix when Todd walked in.

"Who's speaking at this event, Jim?"

I was hoping he knew, but it appeared he really wanted me to earn my money. "David, Elisa, and Garry," I shot back, acting like I had it under control.

"What about Randy? Isn't he part of this one?" Todd asked. Because we were in the middle of a four-city tour with four different groups of speakers, it was easy to forget.

"Hey, I've got the show rundown right here, you guys." Craig, who oversees all things technical at our conferences, fortuitously interrupted our forgetfulness. "Yeah, Randy's on this show. In fact, I just saw him out in the lobby standing behind Jesus. I know he'll be coming in soon because of that tableful of food over there."

"Standing behind Jesus?" I asked.

"You had to be there, Jim," Craig chuckled.

When you work with the variety of venues that we do, you learn to keep your expectations low. The host venue for this conference in Phoenix, however, was Mountain View Lutheran Church, and they were throwing our bell curve off in a serious way. They had the room prepped and the tech team ready to work. Mountain View Lutheran overwhelmed us with hospitality and a motivated cadre of volunteers.

Just before each Outsider Interview, Jim, Craig, and Todd meet with the guests to get to know them and prepare them for the show. **Watch the clip "Backstage with the Outsiders."**

The pre-show dinner with our guests is an important part of how we prepare for each Outsider Interview. Beth

Fitch had recruited all of our guests including Abdo, the only Muslim guest we interviewed in any of the cities.

My phone rang. It was Beth. "He's celebrating Ramadan, Jim." Beth wanted to give me a cultural heads up about our Muslim guest. "He's fasting, so don't offer him any food, and don't give him any money or he will be offended." (We give each guest $50.) "Oh, and he's bringing five friends with him. I hope that's okay."

"Bring 'em all, we have plenty of food," I assured Beth as I quickly scanned the food table and just as quickly remembered they'd all be fasting. "No problem, it'll be fun."

This flurry of activity is typical. Last-minute changes have now become part of the plan. Sometimes one of our guests will get cold feet. Some of them have been talked out of participating by their non-Christian friends on the drive to the venue. They are certain that their friend is walking into some kind of trap we Christians have deviously set. It's all very colorful.

A few minutes later Beth, her Muslim friend Abdo, and his support team walked into the venue.

"Todd, meet Abdo and his friends," she said.

Todd extended his hand and, not having gotten the fasting memo, pulled them toward the food. Beth jumped in to rescue Todd from the cultural faux pas. "Hey Abdo, come over here and meet Craig. He works with Jim and Todd."

Craig sat down with Abdo and company and began to get the backstory on how Abdo got talked into doing this interview. The room was full of energy. It's always this way. Good will, curiosity, and friendship permeate the atmosphere. Helen, who was leading the concierge team that welcomes and connects people, walked in with her warm smile and an armful of materials and said, "Jim, can you guys help me get these brochures folded?" With that, all of us—interviewers, producers, outsiders, and insiders—grabbed some brochures and furiously folded as we talked, ate, and fasted.

We eventually straggled out onto the stage to continue the conversation we'd begun in the dining room. This little group that had formed less than an hour before around a common curiosity about religion, Christianity, and spirituality had already bonded.

Todd launched into the interview with a provocative question. He wanted to know how our guests felt about the strange practice we Christians have developed of calling them *lost* behind their backs. Turning to Erin, he asked, "So, have you heard that famous story about the prodigal son?"

Erin is highly educated and had spent a fair amount of time around Christians when she was in high school and college. You could tell she was working hard to connect with the story. "No, I really don't remember that story, Todd."

Looking for help, Todd turned to Abdo. "How about you, Abdo? Do you know this story?"

Abdo came up blank as well.

Having spent the past ten years asking many people this same question, I was not surprised that our outsider guests had no working knowledge of a story we insiders take for granted. For me, this brief exchange provides a snapshot of the spiritual predicament we find ourselves in. For the past five hundred years, the tectonic plates of socio-spiritual change have been slowly grinding right under our feet. Post-Christendom is no longer something that will happen in the future; it's happening now. Normally the time we "see" an earthquake is when the stuff is falling off the shelves. This awkward moment between Todd, Erin, and Abdo captured my attention in the same way.

Todd could see that Erin had more on her mind and asked her a follow-up question. "Erin, we Christians aren't trying to be mean. How did the language we meant for good come out sounding so bad?"

Erin's been baptized but now discovers there's more. What does it take to be in? **Watch the clip "In or Out? Erin Wants to Know."**

Erin, who during college had succumbed to being baptized in an attempt to satisfy her Christian friends, was wondering why that wasn't enough and why she needed to do something more, such as accepting Jesus as her Savior.

As I listened to Erin and Todd, I found myself wondering how the church let someone like Erin slip through our fingers. It was almost as if we had inoculated her against following Jesus. Even after all the religious influences she'd experienced, she sounded about as interested in God as a lapsed member of an Elks lodge at a recruiting dinner.

As the host of the interviews, I spend a lot of my time *reading the audience.* I pay attention to body language (leaning toward or away from us?) and eye engagement (looking at us or the ceiling?). Experience has taught me that people can only stay engaged for one to two minutes before they get bored or distracted. From all of the signals it was evident that this Mountain View audience had some questions of their own, so we handed them the mic. The first question was aimed at me.

"Jim, earlier in the interview you asked the panel if they'd heard what you called the most widely understood version of the gospel, which you suggested was 'accept Christ and you go to heaven, and if you don't, you go to hell.' Here's my question: why did you frame the question that way? Why not ask them to respond to John 3:16, 'For God so loved the world,' instead?"

The person who asked that question is a very old friend of mine and was one of my first mentors in the faith. Ironically, he was one of the people who had impressed upon me the importance of letting people know they had to make a decision to accept or reject Christ. Fortunately, his influence in my life went beyond his *Left Behind* theology. He and his wife opened their home to hundreds of young people who were coming to faith during the Jesus People days, including me. They lived sacrificially and showed us what following Jesus looks like when it's not a program. Like all of us, he has mellowed with age, which explains why he was trying to get me to reframe my question to the panel so that it was more about how much God loved them and less about hell.

The questions were challenging, so we were actually relieved when the clock rescued us. The three of us are always anxious to get something on paper, but getting away from the venue isn't always that easy. Following the official Q&A is the unofficial Q&A. People are curious. They ask us questions such as, "How did you get these people to agree to do this interview?" and "Why are you so rude by calling them outsiders?" Beth had invited several other friends as well, including a young gay man who had some challenging comments for us, including "I don't know why you think God is against gay people" and other fun topics.

Craig noticed Todd and I were trapped.

We have an agreement that if one of us is being held hostage (conversationally speaking), the other guys will cut in, interrupt, and remind us we have another appointment to get to. It's not a perfect system, but it's good enough. With Craig's help, Todd and I talked our way out the door of Mountain View Lutheran Church.

Normally Phoenix is known for its sunshine, but this weekend it was raining cats and dogs. Being from Seattle, I knew the drill, so I grabbed my coat, pulled it over my head, and made a mad dash for the car. We started driving as Craig checked his iPhone for a list of nearby restaurants. We instructed Craig's phone to lead us to a place in Scottsdale that had happy hour prices starting at nine, and we sloshed our way there.

We unpacked our laptops and ordered some wings. In short order Craig and I had our mouths full, so Todd got us started.

"As I see it, you guys, this interview was all about the blinders we Christians have on when it comes to how we see outsiders."

Craig, who was busy working on his wings, gave me the head nod, so I jumped in. "Yes, for example, Todd, take when you asked Erin and Abdo if they'd ever heard the well-known story of the prodigal son and they responded with a blank look. I realized in that moment that we tend to think that because something is so familiar to us, it must be familiar to everyone."

Todd interrupted. "I was caught off guard by their response but just as quickly became amused by my own assumptions."

69

These after-the-interview conversations are often nothing more than three excited guys interrupting each other with insights, observations, and questions while we eat, drink, and type. Exhibit A: I wanted to hear more of Todd's thoughts about this part of the interview, but I needed to share an experience with him first.

He grabbed a wing and I talked.

"The other day I was talking with someone about renting their venue for a conference I was planning. This was in Seattle, where unlike in the South, small talk doesn't include asking someone where they go to church. Anyway, I'd left a message with our website address on it the day before so they could vet us. The woman I eventually spoke with had visited our website and by the time we got on the phone had determined that I was definitely not an insider in her world. In her mind I was a fanatical Christian. Instead of listening, she gave me a speech. Regardless of how hard I tried, I couldn't get her to listen to my point of view. To play off your theme, Todd, her *insider blinders* were securely attached to her insider head. In that moment I realized that we Christians do exactly the same thing to those we call outsiders."

"Jim, what we experienced tonight was a clear example of the growing awkwardness in the conversation between the church and the wider culture. Erin and Abdo both alerted me to the fact that most outsiders aren't asking for more information; they're asking us 'what's real?'"

Todd, who is a big Lakers fan, glanced at the TV to catch the score.

Craig, seeing the opportunity, jumped in. "How about Erin's question, Jim?"

"Which one?" I shot back, anticipating a trick question coming my way.

"The one about beliefs. Erin seemed like someone who hadn't gotten the memo that being a Christian is not about what you do but what you believe. Is that how you guys see it? And while you're at it, would you mind answering the other question she asked but you didn't answer?"

"Which one?"

"The one about whether you think her sister is going to hell or not."

"Sure, no problem. I'll get to that right after I tell you how many angels can dance on the head of a pin."

"Okay, Craig, all my lame jokes aside, as I see it your question exposes the core issue that informs the whole insider-outsider divide. It's what I call *beliefism*—the worship of right beliefs. Christianity and beliefs have become inseparably connected in our minds. In fact, *believers* is the word evangelical Christians seem to choose most often when asked to describe themselves. Consequently, those who are watching and listening to us, aka outsiders, have come to understand our religion as a set of beliefs or propositions. That's why I traded in the traditional term *Christian* for the term *follower of Jesus*. This term seems to get closer to the process of being a Christian instead of the proposition that determines whether we're in or out."

Craig, who was typing, screeched to a halt. "Jim, I totally relate with what you're saying about beliefism. I know many Christians are concerned about beliefs, but I'm not. Don't get me wrong; this doesn't mean I don't have beliefs. I do; I just don't see the point of defending them."

Craig's lack of interest in defending his beliefs expressed the dilemma a growing number of young Christians talked to us about, so I asked him to unpack his meaning.

"Let's be real, Jim: beliefs are pretty subjective. That's why I have learned to differentiate between beliefs and faith. As I see it, if I knew for a fact that my beliefs were true, then it wouldn't be faith anymore."

"Whoa, hold on, Craig." Todd had a sense of concern in his voice. "Let's not throw the baby out with the bathwater. I can see how you may have come to value faith more than beliefs, but isn't it a little unfair to say that you're not concerned about beliefs? I'd even suggest that it's *because of* your beliefs that you have faith in the first place."

Craig pondered for a moment. I could tell he was really taking Todd's pushback seriously. And then in a more delicate tone he responded, "I think we may be dealing with some nuances in language here, Todd. I'm not sure I hear the word *belief* the same way that you do. To me belief is synonymous with what Jim described earlier as beliefism. Beliefs to me seem to be more about the small things (homosexuality, abortion, etc.) than the big things (God, Jesus, etc.). They seem to be more about knowing what you are against than what you are for. And they seem to be very absolute, not something that you can change your mind about. For all of those reasons, I prefer to use the word *faith*. Faith to me says that I don't know for sure, but I'm putting my money on Jesus. It doesn't mean that I don't believe; it just means that my belief is based on faith. I hear what you are saying about beliefs leading to faith and think that's possible for some people, but that's not been my experience. I realize I'm probably incorrectly using the words *belief* and *faith*.

Todd didn't miss a beat.

"Craig, I do think we're using the word *belief* differently. And for that matter, the way most Christians use the word is actually different from its original meaning. *Believe* in the New Testament has little to do with mental agreement with a proposition. It includes mental 'work' but cannot be reduced to it. That reductionism, I think, is the error that you might be feeling in your guts. In the Bible, *believe* means something like 'place your confidence in.' This is most clearly seen in Jesus's parable at the end of the Sermon on the Mount. After all the amazing teaching in the Sermon, Jesus closes it with: 'If you hear these words of mine and *only use them in Bible studies*, you are like a foolish person who built his or her life on the sand.' But, Jesus said, 'If you hear my words and *place your confidence in them*, if you *act* on them because you believe they are right, good and true, you are like a wise person who built his or her life on the rock.'[1] As I see it, when you separate belief from action, belief loses its original meaning. For example, I can say that I believe flying is the best way to travel, but if I never actually flew anywhere, you would wonder if I really believed that. But if I get on a plane five to ten times a month, you know that I believe in flying.

"One more thing, Craig, before I let you off the hook: you may say you aren't really comfortable with the word *believe*. But I've known you enough years now and watched your life and the way you treat people enough to know that in the sense of 'confidence in Jesus,' in the sense of trying sincerely to 'act' on the Jesus way, you are a 'believer'—deal with it!" Todd finished with a grin.

"Fine!" Craig announced. "If belief was measured by our actions, I wouldn't be so resistant to the word! And then

Christianity wouldn't be known as being hypocritical, because by definition, our beliefs and actions would have to line up. I'll have to think about this more, but I think we're on to something here!"

Keeping his eyes on us, Craig took a sip of beer and moved on to his next point. "You guys still haven't told me how you would answer Erin's question about whether her sister, who's not a believer but serves the poor, is slated for hell or not. *Why is hell so damn important to Christians, anyway?* From my point of view, approaching people with the idea that we think they're going to hell seems like a pretty disrespectful if not impossible way to start a relationship."

"Craig," I said, leaning in, "how many microbrews have you had, anyway? Just kidding!"

Since taking on hell was a bit above my pay grade, I gave Bishop Todd the nod.

"As I see it," Todd began, "we don't get to know one hundred percent of the time who is going where in the life to come. My favorite explanation goes like this: hell is the place God reserved for people who want nothing to do with him; in the end God will simply affirm their desire to have nothing to do with him. I think C. S. Lewis put it this way: 'The door to hell would be locked on the *inside*.' And for what it's worth, I doubt that Erin's sister falls in the category of wanting absolutely nothing to do with God—even if she is struggling with some issues of faith."[2]

Craig appreciated Todd's take. "Thanks for being so straight with me. I wish other leaders in my life had been as forthright. It seems to me that Erin can't understand how God could send her sister to hell for having wrong beliefs while ignoring all the good stuff she does. And you know what? I agree with her. In fact, as I see it, Erin's sister is already walking in the footsteps of Jesus, whether she realizes it or not. I think that as Christians, we need to celebrate *right practice* and not just focus on *right belief*."

Where does morality come from for Outsiders? Is it possible to not know Jesus and be a moral person? **Watch the clip "Can Outsiders Have Morals?"**

"Craig," I responded, "Here's what I've learned about that: when people like each other, the rules change."

"Jim, if you've said that once, you've said it a hundred times."

"I know, but it's true! When you practice being unusually interested in others, they find it hard not to like you. And the practice of being curious and interested in others is what makes dialogue so much friendlier than debate."

"Dialogue isn't as easy as inspirational films like *Remember the Titans* or *Coach Carter* lead us to believe, Jim. My attempts at dialogue have proven to be quite messy at times, especially when I'm attempting to process significant differences with someone."

"Like your dad, Craig?"

"Bingo, Jim! My dad and I have very different ideas about some important topics. I want to be able to talk to him about these things, but too often it just turns into a heated debate. Staying in dialogue has been a messy process for us,

"Only one-third of young outsiders believe that Christians genuinely care about them (34 percent). And most Christians are oblivious to these perceptions—64 percent of Christians said they believe that outsiders would perceive their efforts as genuine."

Kinnaman and Lyons, *unChristian*, 68–69

but we're working on it, which is why I wrote the chapter about our relationship. Another example of what I'm talking about is Klarisa, the young woman we interviewed in Kansas

City who struggled with what to do with an unplanned pregnancy. How would you respond if someone you cared about told you they were considering an abortion, Jim? Could you walk with them, even if their final decision went against your beliefs? That's what I call messy—dialogue is messy."

Glancing at his text messages, Craig kept talking. "It's no wonder most people choose to hide behind the beliefs barricade. It's easier. It virtually guarantees that the people you disagree with will never bother you again. I would like to think that if I were confronted with a situation like Klarisa's, I would be able to walk with that person, help them process their decision, and stand with them regardless of whether or not their final decision concurred with my viewpoint."

I wasn't sure how to respond. I thought about some of the people I'd rejected in the past because they hadn't agreed with my beliefs. I thought about the times I had failed with the Klarisas in my life. Instead of turning to my beliefs as a source of strength, I used them as a weapon on others. Mercifully, Craig interrupted my mental self-flagellation.

"This reminds me, Jim—you seem to collect so many different kinds of friends with all sorts of views and beliefs. Whenever I come over to Seattle to visit you, I get ready to have my mind relationally stretched. How do you manage to remain friends with so many different kinds of people without letting the differences drive you crazy?"

"CBT, Craig."

"Sounds like a pesticide. What's CBT?"

"*C* means *catch* people doing the right thing—something good, usually for others. *B* means *blame* them for being successful. Ask, 'How did you ever think to do that?' *T* means *tell* on them—spread positive gossip about them.

"Basically," I explained, "when it comes to relating with people, you have two choices: you can look for the good or look for the bad. Unfortunately, the stream of Christianity you and I have been most influenced by has taught us to focus on the bad in others. CBT takes the opposite approach. CBT is what Jesus practiced with the centurion, the woman at the well, the woman caught in adultery, and a host of other outsiders—and a few insiders."

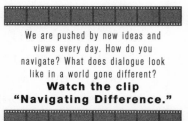

We are pushed by new ideas and views every day. How do you navigate? What does dialogue look like in a world gone different? **Watch the clip "Navigating Difference."**

Being the thoughtful young iconoclast he is, Craig found a chink in my theological armor and came straight at me. "But didn't Jesus catch the woman in adultery, blame her for her sins, and tell her to go and sin no more? Where's the CBT in that?"

Fortunately for me, the Reverend Dr. Hunter heard Craig's question and, averting his eyes from the Lakers game, offered his two theological cents. "Everything is situational, Craig. Yes, sometimes Jesus confronted people and told them to 'go and sin no more,' which we tend to hear as some sort of moralism. But what if it was more like a parent telling a child who just almost got hit by a car to 'go and play, but stay out of the street'—with the emphasis being that the street is bad for kids like adultery is bad for humans? If I am even close to right, it totally changes the tone of the conversation we can have with outsiders.

"And to Jim's CBT thing, it is true that Jesus caught outsiders doing the right thing and then commended them—like Zacchaeus the hated tax collector. Jesus didn't just see Zacchaeus as that horrible person who ripped people off; he also saw the possibilities of who Zacchaeus could be. Dang—I sound like Robert Schuller, talking about possibilities . . ."

While Todd was talking, I was able to organize my own answer for Craig's question.

"Craig, in my first book, *Evangelism without Additives*, I gave one of the chapters this title: 'Ivan Wasn't Always Terrible.' In it I suggest that we insiders have created an image of a God who only has eyes for evil. He seems, at best, neutral to goodness in us or others. But Jesus was able to catch people doing the right thing. In fact, he turned this practice into something of an art form. For example, when Jesus pointed to the Roman centurion and said, 'I have never seen such great faith in all Israel,' he wasn't kidding. He really meant it.[3]

"Jesus, the leader of the revolutionary movement you and I signed up for, made a habit of noticing God wherever God was able to break through—be it in a Jew, gentile, man, woman, or child. He was able to read their hearts and see the goodness of God in them even when they couldn't see it in themselves."

We'd lost Todd. His eyes were glued to the TV. The Lakers were on a roll.

"Todd? Would you like to contribute?"

"Todd!"

"Jim, here's my take. God is like someone whose house just burned down. While stumbling through the remains the next day, he catches a glimpse of a picture of his kids—even through the soot of destruction. Then, reaching down and getting his hands dirty, he picks up the picture with the intention of making it whole again."

"That's what I mean by CBT, you guys. God is looking for the best in people, not the worst. By getting into the beliefs business, the church has gotten out of the God business."

Todd interrupted. "Jim, your characterization seems too harsh—overstated. It's true that the church sometimes has lost sight of the behaviors which beliefs are intended to produce, but not all churches have. Where's your CBT for the church?"

"Sorry, Todd," I conceded. "I was overreacting. It's true that humans need beliefs, what I think you call *beliefs gone good*. What I'm trying to say is that beliefs are designed to guide us, but somehow when they become central, we can become mean. We begin to take the words of Jesus and impose a meaning on them he never intended. All I'm saying is that we've demanded too much from beliefs and too little from love. We need to get beliefs off the deck of the ship and back in the engine room where they belong."

Craig was tapping his beer bottle nervously, a kind of Morse code signaling that he wanted to talk. "Jim, you heard what Brian said in the interview, right? About how God had not created people to be gay?"

"Right, Craig, and not only that, he was really wanting to go after the whole tolerance thing—something I found surprising, considering his age and liberal political leanings."

"Well, you may not have noticed it, but immediately after the show Brian and the gay guy Beth invited got into a pretty intense conversation."

"How did *that* go?" I asked.

"It was so cool! Instead of arguing, they got into a pretty respectful dialogue about God, the Bible, and homosexuality. Last thing I saw was Brian, Beth's gay friend, and some other people heading out to grab a coffee after the interview. I was really impressed with Brian, especially considering how passionately he expressed his beliefs in the interview."

Craig had hit the nail on the head. Somehow Brian had poked enough holes in his belief blinders to enable him to see people out of the corner of his eye. Brian had developed sufficient peripheral vision, spiritually speaking, to allow him to *see* people like this gay man—the same way Jesus saw the Samaritan woman, the centurion, the thief on the cross, and the woman caught in adultery.

"Get you guys anything else?" Our waitress jolted us back to reality. Once again the three of us were in danger of closing down yet another eatery, but we weren't done yet.

"I've been bothered in a good way by something all night," Todd said. "The 'blinders' analogy brought to mind the issue of judging others. Not only is judging wrong, but because all of us have blinders on, we are incapable of accurately judging others. I mean, I still think I should stop someone who's been pounding down one beer after another all night from driving home. That is self-evident. But sometimes it's hard to know where a person is at with God based solely on a brief interview about their beliefs. I'm not talking about people who have seriously considered Christ and rejected him. I'm thinking of the people we encounter every day who are mostly a big blob of confusion about religion, God, Christianity, and Jesus."

"You mean like Erin?" I asked.

"Right, Jim. This interview reminded me once more that people are so much more than their beliefs. Until I get to know someone, I can't see the context out of which those beliefs have developed. That's why I've committed to never reducing someone to their present beliefs and to poke as many holes as I can in my own blinders by entering into genuine conversation with outsiders."

80

"Sounds like our good friend Brian McLaren's mantra, Todd: 'Stop comparing your best with their worst.'"

I heard the beer bottle tapping. Craig wanted the last word.

"Speaking of good friends, Jim, how about Jesus?"

I was a bit surprised with Craig's newfound interest in theology, but not wanting to discourage him, I asked, "Jesus?"

> "Most Christian young people told our interviewers that our faith seems too focused on other people's faults. More than half the young Christians between the ages of sixteen and twenty-nine (53 percent) said they believe that the label *judgmental* accurately fits present-day Christianity."
>
> Kinnaman and Lyons, *unChristian*, 182

Craig seized the opportunity. "Yes, Jesus. He talked about blinders too, you know."

"Where's that, Craig?"

"Matthew 7:5: 'Take the plank out of your own eye, and then you will see clearly how to remove the speck from your brother's eye,'" Craig recited from the NIV.

"Very impressive," I chuckled, "but I'm sure your Sunday school teachers never anticipated you'd be quoting the Bible with a beer in your hand."

5

THE BIG QUESTION

How Did You Get Outsiders to Agree to Do This?

Jim Henderson

What's the question we get asked most? "How did you get the outsiders to agree to participate?"

Even though I know this question is coming, it still catches me off guard because it exposes the not-so-hidden reality that we Christians have drifted so far away from the people Jesus misses most that we think it's difficult to find a couple of them who might be willing to talk.

Don't feel bad—even the professionals can't find them. As part of our preparation for the interviews, we asked pastors to recruit four guests, and even with six months' lead time, many of them were unable to find two outsiders who trusted them enough to get on stage with them.

The reason is simple. In order for people to trust you, they have to know you or know someone who knows you. And the sad fact is that most Christians, especially professional

Christians, have lost touch with outsiders.[1] Our contact with them usually only occurs if they come to our church. So if you approach someone you have no real relationship with and ask them if they would like to be part of an interview you are doing with non-Christians—and oh, by the way, we actually will call you "outsiders"—it's unlikely they will say yes (if they are sane).

But not if you're Kirk Wullf or Beth Fitch.

Kirk and Beth are the people who agreed to help us find the guests for our interviews in Kansas City and Phoenix. I thought hearing how they went about it might prove helpful to those of you who are considering doing this yourself. We think that Outsider Interviews could become a regular part of church life. Imagine the impact if three to four times a year, the congregation experienced an outsider interview. You could interview teenage outsiders, women outsiders, immigrant outsiders, senior outsiders, outsiders of other faiths, and the list goes on and on. Eventually people in the church would suggest people they would like to hear from, plus it would be a very cool meeting to bring their own outsider friends to. Imagine the impression it would make on them to see a church that actually listens to people who don't attend. They would be shocked and forced to remove you from their dumb church list.

But let's get back to Beth and Kirk.

Beth: The Great Connector

As I mentioned in the previous chapter, Beth Fitch took responsibility for finding our four guests for the interview in Phoenix.

Beth is a lawyer and a very active follower of Jesus. She knows lots of Christians and non-Christians. She is comfortable interacting with people who are on the path toward faith as well as those who aren't. She is connected with a large network of Christians who are interested in the same thing, which is why she was able to take on this unusual assignment.

I asked Beth about her experience.

"Because I know loads of outsiders, I thought it would be a no-brainer, Jim, but then you raised the bar with 'I need a Muslim between the ages of nineteen and thirty.' I do know a few Muslims, but not in that age range. So I put word out to my network, and soon I was on the phone with Abdo, a young man from Yemen who is now selling cars here in Phoenix. Abdo heard about the interview through the daughter of a friend and agreed to do it as a favor to her. He was quite comfortable with the whole idea but told me that he would not be eating until after dark since it was Ramadan, plus he wanted to bring five Muslim friends along. Given all our country has gone through since 9/11, you can imagine I had some anxiety about five Muslims showing up on a church campus. It sounds weird, but I was actually afraid that some Christians might act inhospitably toward them, so I arrived early to meet them before the show and escorted them to the pre-show dinner."

Beth's comment about inhospitable Christians could not have been less true about the folks at Mountain View Lutheran. They were warm and welcoming, but I understood her anxiety. As Kinnaman's research uncovered, we Christians have become so closely associated with politics that we are a bit unpredictable to outsiders.

Kirk: The Starbucks Pastor

Kirk was responsible for finding four people for the Kansas City interview (the first one in this book). He is on staff at Christ Church and is one of the best I have ever met at connecting with outsiders. Kirk has even written spending time with outsiders into his job description. He schedules something like 25 percent of his office time at a local Starbucks, practicing what he calls "hanging out." He reads the paper or writes and simply *notices* people. Due to the sheer amount of time he puts in, as well as his welcome smile and willingness to talk, Kirk is never short on conversations. In fact, they have now designated him the official pastor at this Starbucks. As a result of this intentionality, Kirk has accumulated more relationships with outsiders than he can keep up with.

Explaining what we are trying to accomplish in the interviews to a group of Christians is hard enough, but trying to explain it to non-Christians is even more difficult. Their first response is usually skepticism and distrust. They've never heard of a church that truly wanted to hear their opinions, no strings attached. The outsiders who do agree to participate often do so as a favor to someone like Kirk, who is typically the one Christian they do trust. The person issuing the invitation is taking a significant risk as well. It's all very precarious, like walking a tightrope, which is what makes it so much fun. People like Kirk are the key connectors in these networks of relationships. They establish deep trust and demonstrate exquisite restraint by practicing love as often as possible and by not preaching when they're tempted to.

Kirk worked hard to pull together the interview team, and then at the last minute one of the outsiders got cold feet and called in sick, leaving Kirk scrambling. Thanks to his deep reserves of relational capital, Kirk was able to get on the phone and within thirty minutes locate two more outsiders who were willing to show up as a favor to a friend of Kirk's. It was very impressive to watch and frankly a profoundly spiritual process to observe. Kirk was even able to use the cancellation to reconnect with the person who had dropped out.

Kirk told me what happened as a result of him checking back with the person who cancelled.

"Jim, the person who cancelled on me a few hours before the show later ended up traveling to Uganda with me and some others from Christ Church. And get this: despite her roommate's warnings prior to her traveling with us, she chose to follow Christ."

Kirk had known she would be feeling bad about canceling, so he revisited her to assure her that everything went well with the interview. This gesture served to deepen her trust in Kirk. She knew she wasn't a target or a project. That furthered her resolve to travel with Kirk and his team to Africa, where she came to a personal encounter with Jesus.

Did you catch that? Kirk and his team brought outsiders with them *on their mission trip*. How innovative is that?

One of our guests in Kansas City was Klarisa. People often ask us what happens to the interviewees after the interview. Kirk sent us this update on Klarisa a couple of months after we were there.

"Jim, the Klarisa story is getting more interesting every day. What's really cool is that she's joined Alpha now and loves it. We're continuing to unpack the damage done by the past. She's amazing. Her life is so different now than it was at the time of the interview! She's still not a Christian, but the Spirit is drawing her closer to Jesus every day. And she trusts and genuinely loves all the folks from our Alpha group who are in her life. Just thinking about this journey enlarges my heart so much."

Kirk's note continued, and he made me promise to print the following:

"One more thing, Jim. People need to know that in no way did I view Klarisa or my other friends at Starbucks as 'projects.' I just wanted to be intentional in getting to know more people outside the church and to perhaps bring the perspective, hope, goodness, and beauty of Jesus to a place like Starbucks. Even though we have grown kids ourselves, Klarisa has become like a daughter to my wife Diana and me. She spent Christmas at our home, she's been to the house to watch University of Kansas basketball games, and she hung out with us during the Super Bowl. It's been an honor for me to have her trust. She is still exploring Christianity, but we will be friends *even if she decides to stop her pursuit of Christianity*. Jesus loves her so much, and he has enlarged my heart for her and so many others who are outside the church. My motivation is for her to know just how much Jesus loves her and cares for her and wants the very best for her."

The Connectors

Beth and Kirk are what I call *connectors*. Connectors might replace traditional evangelists in the coming decades. Here's why. Evangelists have *speaking* skills; connectors have *listen-*

ing skills. Evangelists *win* people to Christ; connectors *woo* people to Christ. Evangelists understand *apologetics*; connectors understand *apologies*. Evangelists engage in *debates*; connectors in *dialogue*. Finally, evangelists count *conversions*; connectors count *conversations*.

Most significantly, Beth and Kirk have learned that when it comes to connecting with people who have a skewed image of God or who have closed themselves off from God, the two most important questions are not "If you died right now, do you know for sure you'd go to heaven?" or "If you were standing before God and he said, 'Why should I let you into heaven?' what would you say?"

The two most important questions are "How are you?" and "How are Chris and the kids?"

Have you noticed that you haven't been able to change your basic personality structure? You are who you are. Because of Jesus, you are hopefully a better version of yourself than you were without his help, but you still possess the same personality. Trying to become someone other than who you are is simply a waste of time. That means you are not me or Beth or Kirk. You are you.

Since God has asked us to connect with and serve outsiders, he must be prepared to do it through each one of us in a unique way. That's what we mean by *really personal evangelism*. The only other logical conclusion available (and the one that has been the default mode for the past fifty years) is that this is a job for specialists (aka evangelists). Since that is not a biblically plausible solution and since most of us seem to retain an urge to serve and connect with outsiders, we need to find doable spiritual practices that enable us to connect with outsiders in normal ways.

I've been experimenting with spiritual practices that enable us to connect with the people Jesus misses most for almost fifteen years. After watching Kirk and Beth and Todd and others, I've come up with a simple list of things *you are already doing* that will lead you to connect with outsiders if you just do them a little more intentionally. That wasn't a misprint—I said things you are *already doing*, not things you need to learn how to do.

People change when you give them something to do that they are already doing. We adopt new technologies like smartphones because we already know how to use a cell phone. We adopted the cell phone because it was a portable version of something we already knew how to use, the home phone. We adopted iPods because they are a high tech version of the Sony Walkman, which was an improved version of the cassette player, which was a portable version of the tape recorder in our homes.

Kirk and Beth are doing things you and I *already know how to do*. The only difference: they do them on purpose.

The Power of Like

The most important spiritual practice Kirk and Beth have perfected is something profoundly simple but radically different. Simply put, they have moved beyond love into like.

Saying God loves people is easy. I like to joke that God has to love people in order to keep his job. Theologians explain it by saying his nature *is* love. Do you love people you don't really like all that much? We all do. But when I say I like someone, I mean I admire, respect, and enjoy them. I'm interested in what they like and dislike. I enjoy their company.

Four Things You Already Know How to Do

1. Notice People

Everything we need is right in front of us. If we look closely enough, we will see things that others don't see. My wife calls this seeing people "out of the corner of your eye." All connecting begins with noticing.[2]

"Klarisa was sitting at a table with an enormous binder full of material in front of her. I simply asked, 'What are you looking at?'"—Kirk

2. Be Curious

We long for people to be interested in us. There's something about someone *inquiring* into our lives and thinking that helps us make better decisions. Being curious is a spiritual practice for Beth and Kirk.

"Klarisa said she was studying to be a shift supervisor and she needed to learn everything in the book. Our friendship started with that small question. I've learned that small talk is a natural on-ramp for the opportunity for deeper conversation."—Kirk

3. Be Intentional but Not Manipulative

When I ask people why they don't evangelize, the number one reason is they don't like manipulating their friends. Kirk and Beth have learned the spiritual practice I call non-manipulative intentionality – which means the practice of being intentional without being manipulative.

"At the grocery store I request the 'bagger' to help me take my groceries to the car. I always engage in conversation. The first question is usu- ally *'How are you?' Most people don't expect you to sincerely care about the answer. When I follow up with a more in-depth question, these kids begin to really open up. I have chatted with kids in the grocery parking lot about things from school failures to dysfunctional families to friends' suicides."—Beth*

4. Practice the Golden Rule

The easiest way to connect with outsiders is to practice this: do unto others as you would have them do unto you. That one rule is the only "program" you will ever need. I estimate that upwards of 90 percent of all evangelism programs violate the Golden Rule. Here's what I mean:

Do you like being thought of as a project?

Do you like it when a friend turns out to actually be a salesperson?

Do you like being talked down to?

Do you like it when your opinion is wrong (a lot)?

Seriously, think about how simple this is. It would explain why the majority of Christians persistently stonewall evangelism programs. Perhaps they have been obeying the Spirit all this time while those of us who are paid to be Christians have been attempting to talk them into acting against Jesus's words about loving people the way you would like to be loved. What if history proves them right? Some of us think we may be on the threshold of discovering just that.

Has anyone ever asked you to explain the gospel and given you about thirty seconds to do so? I started experimenting with different responses beginning with the tried and true *God loves you* angle, but that didn't seem to impact people all that much, probably because we've said it so many times on TV, bumper stickers, and bad church signs. But when I started asking people the question "What if there was a God who liked you—would that be good news?" their eyes lit up. This has become my short form explanation of the gospel: *Jesus is the God who likes people.* I realize this may not satisfactorily address the issue of sin for some, but neither does it shut down the conversation.

Both Kirk and Beth reminded me numerous times that they actually *like* the outsiders with whom they connect. Beth said, "Because I am genuinely interested in hearing their stories, people open up. I also try to relate to them. If I have had an experience that is similar to their experience, I share it. This creates a bond and leads to deeper sharing by them."

Kirk said, "I would show acts of kindness not expecting anything else in return. I remember one time when I had $50 left on my prepaid Starbucks card. It was April 16, the end of tax season. I gave the card to one of the baristas and told her to use it up buying drinks for people going through the drive-through to celebrate the end of tax day. Not only did the patrons appreciate it (some even wanted to fill out a comment card), but the baristas appreciated the act of kindness. I think it gave me credibility with them."

And don't think for a minute Beth and Kirk don't care whether people become followers of Jesus—they do. Kirk said, "Jesus loves Klarisa so much, and he has enlarged my heart for her and so many others who are outside the church.

My motivation is for her to know just how much Jesus loves her and cares for her and wants the very best for her. Jesus has chosen me to bring that message to her and hopefully to many, many others."

And Beth said, "John is my personal trainer at Lifetime Fitness. We have spent hours together and talk about everything. He was an easy choice for an outsider interview we did one Sunday morning at church. When he was in the church lobby right after the interview, one of his clients, R.J., came up to him and said he did a great job. R.J. is theologically trained. John and R.J. then began a dialogue about Christianity. John decided he would start reading the Bible but needed some direction, so he mentioned that to R.J. Now R.J. gives John Bible reading assignments and they meet to talk about the assignments. John says he still doesn't believe in organized religion and isn't interested in going to church, but he wants to know more about the Bible. John told me that he talks about the interview pretty regularly. He said it was a fantastic experience for him."

What has changed for Beth and Kirk is this: while they remain passionately committed to seeing their friends become heartfelt followers of Jesus, they will not coerce, manipulate, or violate those friendships to accomplish that goal. The reason Kirk and Beth can make that commitment is because they have discovered the power of *like*. Kirk and Beth have discovered that *when people like each other, the rules change.*

The Backside of Like

But liking people can cut both ways. It sure did for me.

John and I became friends in high school. He was trying to be a Christian at the time, and I did my part to help move him in the opposite direction. I turned him onto jazz and saved him from Young Life. Following high school we both began doing what was normal for us at that time—smoking pot. Since I was a musician, this went with the territory, but I needed to keep a day job, so I limited my drug use to pot and wine. I was happy and told myself I would never shoot drugs intravenously. I liked John and admired his intelligence and coolness.

John and I shared an apartment for a while. I walked into the kitchen one afternoon just as John was "tying off." The meth was in the needle, and he was about to load up. I'd never seen this up close so I watched with rapt attention. He invited me to join him and I did. Just like that I forgot my promise to myself and followed John into serious drug use, just like he had followed me away from Young Life.

I ended up shooting drugs and selling them for a few months until I finally dropped it all. It was getting in the way of my ability to play music, which was of greater importance to me, so I stopped. I was fortunate I didn't get hooked.

From that point on I realized I could never again say *I would never do something* because I had proven that given the right influence, I really could.

The point I want to make is this: because I respected and admired John, I casually dropped what I perceived to be my deeply held beliefs, picked up the needle, and shot dope. There was no long discussion, and he never tried to coerce me. I just did it.

As we can see from watching Beth and Kirk, this influence can be used for good as well as evil. That's because *when people like each other, the rules change*—for good or bad.

It turns out that Jesus can take our no-frills lives and make them effective. He can take our small efforts to connect with outsiders and multiply the meaning of them the same way he multiplied the five loaves and two fish. He doesn't need much, he just needs us to *do something on purpose*. That's all that Kirk and Beth are trying to tell us. And that's all outsiders like Erin are telling us they need—someone who will notice, be curious, and not manipulate them.

They know you want them to know Jesus. That isn't what offends them. What bothers them is that we go about it in inauthentic and not-so-normal ways. What bothers them is that while preaching at them about Jesus, we fail to live like Jesus.

> "Eighty-five percent of young outsiders conclude that present-day Christianity is hypocritical. Half of young churchgoers agreed that Christianity is hypocritical (47 percent)...."
>
> "Overall, 30 percent of born-again Christians admitted to at least one type of sexually inappropriate behavior in the past thirty days, including online pornography, viewing sexually explicit magazines or movies, or having sex outside of marriage, compared with 35 percent of other Americans...."
>
> "Among young outsiders, 84 percent say they personally know at least one committed Christian. Yet just 15 percent thought the lifestyles of those Christ followers were significantly different from the norm."
>
> Kinnaman and Lyons,
> *unChristian*, 42, 47, 48

6

DENVER OUTSIDERS

Diversity and Difference

Jim Henderson

This chapter correlates with the video titled
"Diversity and Difference"
in the Denver section of your DVD.

Kathy Escobar and Karl Wheeler lead The Refuge, a missionally inclined faith community in Denver. A couple of years ago Kathy, Karl, and several carloads of Refuge-ites caravanned over to Seattle to experience an Off The Map conference. They loved it and asked if we could do something similar in Denver. We said yes! Kathy and Karl are highly respected in the Denver area and asked Foothills Community Church to sign on as co-hosts for the conference there.

The Denver show included Todd Hunter, David Kinnaman, Sally Morgenthaler, Randy Siever, Matt Casper, and

Kathy Escobar. But my favorite performer was Sage. Sage plays a desperately funky steel guitar and along with a few other bands set the musical tone for the event. We suggest for these events that people bring their laptops so they can write emails, blog, or use Facebook or Twitter to their hearts' content. Technologically speaking, we decided if we can't beat 'em, we'd join 'em.

Following the main stage interview, Craig and his team shot several hours of one-on-one interviews. That's why a lot of our writing takes place pretty late at night. Todd and I hung around for a bit and then headed back to the hotel and set up with our laptops in the bar adjacent to the lobby.

I arrived first and was checking the menu when David Kinnaman happened by. "Dude, what are you up to?" he asked.

David holds a very impressive title: president of the Barna Group. Nevertheless he remains an unvarnished (*and* incredibly bright) thirty-four-year-old. That night he was wearing a baseball cap, jeans, and red Converse high-tops. Not wanting to appear my age, I shot back, "What are *you* up to, dude? I mean, you're the famous guy!"

Dave was excited. "Have you heard of The Fray, Jim?" I nodded a fake yes. "It turns out the lead singer Isaac lives here in Denver and wants to meet up—how cool is that?"

"Pays to write a bestseller, Dave."

"No, Jim, get this—Isaac is a follower of Jesus and really cares about the stuff you and I are talking about."

Just then Isaac walked in, looking all rock star-ish, meaning compared to me he was incredibly skinny. "Jim, meet Isaac." Even though I'm a musician and know a few formerly famous people, I still get stoked to meet people *while* they're famous.

We shook hands, exchanged greetings, and with that my two most currently famous friends headed for the door.

One of the maxims I live by is "always ask." I train leaders to practice asking people for help. So working up my courage, I shouted, "Hey, Isaac!" The revolving door stuck open. "You need to come to our gig tomorrow and meet my friend Matt Casper, the atheist guy I wrote a book with, *Jim and Casper Go to Church*. He has a killer band called Hell Yeah and would love to meet you."

Much to my surprise, Isaac responded, "I'll be there." And with that he and Dave climbed into the back of his jet black stretch limo (okay, it was a Honda) and drove off into the Denver night.

Todd walked in as they walked out. "Who was that, Jim?"

"Ever heard of The Fray?"

"Umm . . . wait a minute . . . my daughter loves those guys."

"Well, don't tell her, but you just missed getting the lead singer's autograph by about thirty seconds."

"She's gonna kill me."

"No worries, Todd; God provides. I think you'll get a second chance tomorrow. Isaac said he wanted to meet Casper, so I think he'll show up for that session."

Todd was amused. "Pays to know a famous atheist."

Todd and I made our way to the bar (we actually do go to regular restaurants sometimes, but at this time of night most of them are closed). Todd loves Mexican, so he got the $4.95 nachos and I got the sliders for $5.50. Late-night prices!

They brought my rum and Coke and Todd's iced tea. Even though Craig hadn't shown up yet, I decided to get the conversation started. "Todd, Rio's enthusiastic, unabashed way of articulating a deeply personal issue disarmed the audience and really moved me. At times it felt like she was saying, 'If you didn't know I was gay, you'd think I was the most "on fire" Christian on this stage.' I mean, when was the last time any of us had to sit on stage in front of complete strangers and describe, explain, or defend our sexuality? Sometimes I think Christians think about sex more than any other group on the planet. We just can't get enough—especially when it's at someone else's expense."

Todd's theological wheels were already spinning. I could see it in his eyes. "Jim, it's certainly true that we Christians don't have the greatest public reputation on this topic. In fact, it was Kinnaman's stats on this very issue that provoked *The Outsider Interviews*. But if I may (pardon the pun) play devil's advocate on behalf of Christians for just a moment, I think the average Christian, while still holding a view contrary to Rio's, is probably way more tolerant and loving than the few ugly ones we see on the nightly news. Keep in mind that the vast majority of American Christians are trying to deal with beliefs that have consequences in the sexual, political, social, religious, and business aspects of their lives. Actually, Jim, when it comes to homosexuality, compared with religions in other parts of the world, American Christians can appear downright tolerant!"

> "A majority of born-again Christians, including more than four out of five evangelicals, say that homosexual relations between two consenting adults should be illegal."
>
> Kinnaman and Lyons, *unChristian*, 94

Craig showed up in the middle of Todd's apologetic. "Todd, I agree most Christians think their actions are tolerant and loving, but nearly every homosexual I've talked with has had some negative treatment from someone in the Christian community. I wonder if the 'love' that some people think they are giving is actually being received negatively. For instance, is trying to 'fix' someone's homosexuality loving? I'm sure that's received quite differently on the other end. It seems to me that many Christians worry that expressing acceptance will be interpreted as endorsing what they view is immoral. But it's hard for the gay community to feel loved when they certainly aren't accepted."

Noticing that a third party had been seated, our waitress cut in. "Can I get you something?"

"Whatever microbrew you have on tap works for me," Craig said, picking away at Todd's nachos.

Anxious to get our attention off the beer and back to the Bible, Todd broke in, "Craig, there's a passage in the Gospel of Mark that I think might help. In the New Testament, a fig tree symbolizes Israel—the people of God. When Jesus approaches the tree expecting to find fruit and finds none, he curses it—meaning he curses Israel's failure to be the people of God. I think Jesus may very well curse the lack of love as well as the hate toward homosexuals in parts of the church today. Jesus expects his people to bear fruit. In the New Testament the best fruit is always love. In our context here we mean love for gay, lesbian, bisexual, and transgendered persons."

Todd noticed our waitress was nowhere to be found. "Maybe she overheard our conversation and it put her off?"

I suggested that it might be our three laptops, tableful of food, and intense talking that was scaring her. We concluded that as men we were probably completely misreading her.

Getting back to the topic, I added, "Guys, it seems to me that when people like Rio and Andrew with deeply held differences attempt to communicate, debate often ensues. Christians call it 'defending the faith,' which is often code for intellectual holy war. Makes me think of that passage where Peter says 'don't use your freedom as a cover-up for evil' (see 1 Peter 2:16).

"What if instead of defending the faith we chose to 'defend the space'—the sacred space God gives us in opening up a relationship with people who think and act differently than we do. This is why we're doing these interviews and why we decided to mix outsiders and insiders together. We want to see what happens especially among young people when difference shows up."

Craig chimed in. "I agree, Jim, and I know after reading some of my earlier comments people may find it hard to believe, but sometimes even I want to defend the faith and win the religious debate. I guess I revert back to the conservative culture values that were ingrained in me as a kid. But defending your position and winning debates is easy." We all nodded in agreement as Craig made his point: "Maintaining your beliefs while finding commonality in the midst of difference is very, very hard."

> "Out of twenty attributes that we assessed, both positive and negative, as they related to Christianity, the perception of being antihomosexual was at the top of the list. More than nine out of ten Mosaic and Buster outsiders (91 percent) said 'antihomosexual' accurately describes present-day Christianity."
>
> Kinnaman and Lyons,
> unChristian, 92–93

"I hear you," Todd affirmed. "I really believe something is shifting in our world. And just as you've talked about, Jim, our cultural maps are being redrawn right in front of us.

When people get new maps, they get new imaginations. For some it's energizing, but for others it's terrifying. I hope we can calm people's fears by humanizing this process through our guests' stories."

Wanting to make sure we weren't drifting too far afield, I reminded Todd and Craig about the data we found in *un-Christian*. "According to Kinnaman, the highest-ranking negative perception outsiders have of Christians is that we're anti-gay. And what's even more interesting or concerning (depending on your viewpoint) is that 80 percent of young Christians agreed with this assessment. In fact, on most questions the gap between outsiders and insiders was not nearly as great as it would have been thirty years ago, I suspect.

The topic of homosexuality also came up in our Kansas City interview. **Watch the clip "Insiders and Gay People."**

"When I signed up with Jesus there was an *us* and a *them*. We knew who was *in* and who was *out*. And thanks to Hal Lindsey, we also *knew* that the world was going to end soon. We didn't have to know much about other religions because they were nowhere to be found. No one was gay (or at least no one admitted it), global warming was way off in the future, there was no internet to inform us of how other people lived, and no one had a cell phone they could use for instant messaging, Tweeting, or watching YouTube. Being a Christian was straightforward—at least for those of us with long hair, no permanent jobs, and a Jesus rock band to play in.

"Todd, you remember the Jesus People days: 'We've got that blessed belief that baffles the Buddhists.' Now everyone seems so buddy-buddy. Do we blame it all on the devil? Post-

Christendom? Postmodernism? Brian McLaren? How did we get from there to here? Why are insiders identifying with outsiders instead of calling them to repentance like we used to do in the old days?"

Todd's response was simple and profound: "One word, Jim: *pain*. Given enough strength and time, pain always causes change. Its alterations can be good or bad. I see the church in pain, having lost its privileged position in society. I also see hurt over the fear of being judged by outsiders as being narrow-minded, misogynistic, anti-gay, and judgmental. The fact is that none of us like being labeled."

Sam and Charlie discuss their reactions to insider and outsider labels.
Watch the clip "Damaged by Labels."

"That brings up an interesting story for me," Craig shared. "A few months ago, I gave my dad a copy of *unChristian*. After reading the first couple chapters, he told me he didn't understand what the big deal was about labels. He said, 'I'm tired of having to switch labels every few years because it hurts their feelings.' The ease with which he distanced himself from 'them' hurt because I frequently find myself identifying more with outsiders than I do with insiders. And speaking of labels, I have a new category I've created for myself as a result of this project: *insider-outsiders*."

I was interested. "What's an insider-outsider, Craig?"

Craig explained, "Insider-outsiders identify with the core values of Christianity but also find themselves holding views that are deemed ungodly by fellow Christians. Sometimes just associating with the wrong people is enough to gain you temporary outsider status. It frustrates me that I was taught the practice of placing others on a spectrum of faith. What makes this project so interesting to me is that lately in my spiritual journey I've found myself drifting further afield from those insider views, yet ironically I feel closer to God than ever before. The problem is that I love to ask questions. I love to probe other people's assumptions. And I'm learning how to become comfortable with the tension of not knowing things for certain.

When does a slippery slope become a ski jump? Rio and Andrew discuss remaining openhanded with convictions. **Watch the clip "Remaining Open."**

"For example, unlike Todd, I really don't know what I believe about homosexuality. On the one hand it doesn't seem to make a whole lot of sense to me, but when I get beyond the stigmas I was taught, it doesn't feel all that wrong either. Frankly, I don't feel like I have to decide if homosexuality is right or wrong anymore. It just doesn't matter. What I am certain about," Craig continued, "is that God wants me to treat gay people with respect and love. The really big difference between me and *insider-insiders* is that I am open to encountering God in the strangest places regardless of moral purity or unusual beliefs."

Another topic that insider-outsiders don't feel like they have to resolve is abortion. **Watch the clip "Insider Women on Abortion."**

I liked Craig's play on words. "Nice wordsmithing, Craig. It really captures the dilemma both sides feel. It seems Rio has certainly blurred the lines we like to draw between insiders and outsiders."

Todd, who was intensely pecking away on his Dell, suddenly stopped. "As Rio was telling her story, I was watching Andrew, who, given his impressive résumé with Child Evangelism Fellowship, came across as a very serious Christian. I was impressed with his ability to stay connected with Rio even when her story took a sharp turn. In many ways I think Andrew represents the feelings of many young evangelicals—settled in their beliefs but activist in their faith."

I was still thinking about Craig's new category of insider-outsider, which reminded me of something Sam had said. "Sam's self-description as a 'non-Christian Christian' humorously captured his resistance to labels. He impressed me with his intelligence and nuanced way of seeing himself as part of the Christian story while not being a Christian. Alex was interesting because she was brought up in a New Age kind of spirituality, which proved not to be enough to satisfy her desire for a personal god. Her conversion by shooting star was pretty cool, but for my money, Rio's story provided the gravitational pull for the entire show—not only what she said but how she said it."

Is Sam saved? Are his views of morality unbiblical? What does he get right? **Watch the clip "Non-Christian Christian."**

"I was impressed by the way they listened respectfully to each other," Craig replied. "I've been in conversations like this with Christian leaders who would fidget, talk over each other, dominate, and talk down to others. These folks' body language was pretty open, and they were working at supporting each other. Sam could have been more dominant, but he was direct without being overbearing or using his body to control the conversation. Did you guys pick up on that?"

"Yeah," Todd agreed. And then he added enthusiastically, "That reminds me of a Six Degrees of Separation connection I may have with Sam. As he was talking about growing up in Santa Ana, California, it occurred to me that my younger brother, who is now a deputy chief of police in Anaheim and has had extensive experience with gangs, could have had direct or indirect contact with him, but from the other side of the bars. It is a small world with only a few degrees of separation. Being born the right color matters in our culture and has lots to do with who gets advantages and who doesn't."

"Todd, speaking of being born the right color," I added, "I thought that in many ways Andrew's conservative Christian pedigree represented the polar opposite of Sam's. Andrew's the kind of young person Christian parents would like their kids to grow up to be—self-assured, giving, clean-cut, and polite. Almost like an All-American Christian. But all kidding aside, what impressed me most about Andrew was his ability to lean in and listen when Rio started telling her story."

"I agree, Jim. I was very impressed with Andrew's ability to model what it looks like to hold his beliefs and still stay in relationship with those who disagree with him."

"Right, Todd, like when Andrew described the difference between disagreeing with someone in theory versus seeing them face-to-face."

Craig jumped in with one of my favorite expressions. "Jim, is that why you're always saying that when people like each other, the rules change?"

Craig, the famous Chinese General, Sun Tzu, puts it this way: 'The one incalculable in war is the will of the people.'"

"Meaning what?"

"What I mean, Craig, is no matter how many biblical smart bombs you drop down someone's soul chimney, ultimately it all comes down to whether or not they *like* you. If they like you, they will be more open to your ideas, and if they don't, they won't. I've discovered that when two people like Rio and Andrew appreciate, respect, and like each other, the rules change. We don't have to defend the faith; we begin defending the sacred space between us."

"What you call 'defending the space,'" Todd chimed in, "I call 'centered-set faith.'"

"What's that look like, Todd?"

"It comes from social set theory developed by Dr. Paul Hiebert, who suggests that human beings tend to organize themselves in one of three ways: fuzzy sets, centered sets, and bounded sets. I'm only concerned with the bounded and centered sets."[1]

Todd grabbed a napkin and drew two sketches, something like this:

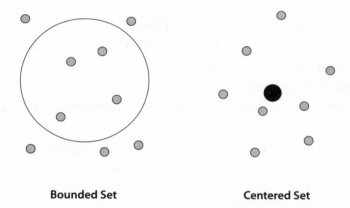

Bounded Set   **Centered Set**

"In bounded sets, the main focus is on the boundary, on answering the question 'Who's in and who's out?' As far back as I can remember, evangelicals have used bounded-set thinking. Conversely, centered-set thinking asks, 'Who's moving toward the center, and who's moving away from the center?'

"I would argue that what we're seeing in someone like Alex, for example, is a follower of Jesus who has stopped asking the who's in and who's out question and has begun instead to practice centered-set faith. What she notices is anyone who is *moving toward* Jesus. As I see it, Jim, we need to capture this new way of being Christian if we intend to help leaders and parents understand the young people they are seeking to influence for the kingdom."

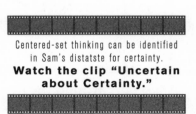

Centered-set thinking can be identified in Sam's distatste for certainty.
Watch the clip "Uncertain about Certainty."

I was, as they say, picking up what Todd was laying down. "I think this helps explain a major spiritual shift that is occurring among young people. Alex and even Andrew seem to be exchanging brand loyalty for community loyalty. All our guests seemed to find a way to connect with each other regardless of the differences."

Since the midnight hour was upon us, Craig was starting to drift off a bit, so I decided to get him reconnected with the conversation. "Craig, one of my favorite moments in this show happened when I was asking Alex about her relationship with Jesus and she responded with a very simple gesture—she touched her heart. For some reason that simple act was so authentic, words weren't necessary. How about you, Craig? Anything make your moment-ology meter?"

Craig thought about it for a minute. "Yeah, and actually it was another Alex moment. In our post-show interview I asked how her Christian friends responded to her more liberal/progressive views. She replied by saying she feels like they often just dismiss her,

Alex shares what it feels like to be on the receiving end of judgment from Christians.
Watch the clip "Democrat Christian Oxymoron?"

but something beneath her words told me that there was more. I asked the question again, and for a moment she let her guard down and I understood her pain. I've felt that same pain myself. Listening to Alex reminded me that ironically, it's sometimes our devotion to follow Christ that exposes us to pain from other Christians."

I nodded in agreement. "One of the most confusing things for people watching and reading this will be how fluid everyone seems around the issue of morality. Once Rio came out with her story, the whole conversation seemed to flow in, around, and through the topic of morality. It appears to me that one of the sea changes that is taking place is that morality is starting to come under greater scrutiny. Up to this point it has been the socio-spiritual property of evangelicals; now all of a sudden non-Christians and outsiders are questioning our narrow definition of the topic. And they're using the words of Jesus to challenge us.

"For example, Sam isn't a Christian, at least in the way we evangelicals describe it, but he definitely sees himself as being in the morality business. Yet he isn't nearly as concerned about sexual morality as he is societal morality. Remember when he talked about Christians giving themselves permission to care about global issues like AIDS while ignoring its local impact?

"And Alex is a follower of Jesus, but she wants to broaden the conversation about morality to include how we treat outsiders instead of just how sexually moral we are. I'm sure this is quite disturbing to those people who are still attempting to navigate using old maps. We've been told if we get too close to sinners, we risk becoming like them, and we have been told that if we hang out with nonbelievers, we need to have an answer for them. But what if they aren't asking the questions we've been trained to answer?"

110

Todd offered an interesting insight. "Jim, for Jesus, morality was never an abstraction. It was a concrete reality that had to do with alignment to the ultimate intention of God. This is what allowed Jesus to hang with various sinners and prostitutes. When pressed about these things his standard answer was: 'I only do and say what I see and hear from my Father.' For Jesus, morals were always rooted in the story of God."

Our waitress was hovering and seemed anxious for us to wrap things up. It was already after midnight, so she probably wanted to get us out the door. I handed her my credit card and asked for one more refill.

Craig had been listening intently. "I really appreciate that perspective, Todd. Viewing morality as being black and white doesn't resonate with my experience . . . but I'm also not comfortable with ignoring morality altogether."

Craig kept going. "Another fascinating interaction with Rio took place after the show when I was interviewing her offstage. She shared more about her fight to resist homosexuality and about crying in the prayer chapel, going to counseling, and attempting to 'de-gayify' herself in other ways. It wasn't like she was parading around campus flipping off the church. At that time *she really didn't want to be gay.* I guess I've always assumed that if you're gay, you're proud of it. She also shared with me that just like straight single people, she struggles with boundaries in the physical aspects of her relationships. Rio is okay with having relationships with other women yet still sees a need for healthy boundaries. I think many insiders

Rio explores the complex world of moral codes. Guilt is part of it, but is it for the right thing? **Watch the clip "Gay Guilt and God."**

would be intrigued to discover that Rio hasn't abandoned her morality.

"To be perfectly honest, you guys, I wonder how the gay issue made the Top Ten on the greatest sins list while other ones like adultery, gluttony, and cheating are widely ignored. Why do we focus so much on homosexuality?

"Just to keep it real and personal . . . several years ago I got married, but within the first year I realized it wasn't going to work, and although it was painful, I decided to initiate a divorce. Since many of my family and friends are Christians and the Bible clearly says that 'God hates divorce,' I expected significant backlash. But to my surprise, I barely encountered any pushback. With the exception of one or two people, everyone was incredibly loving and accepting of my decision. For some reason, the Bible's clarity on divorce was overlooked. Looking back, I wonder if people would have responded the same had I announced that I was gay? I'm guessing not. Don't get me wrong; I think I made the right decision and that God was in my decision and that people responded appropriately. I just wonder why homosexuality is treated so differently."

As I was signing the receipt for our dinner, Todd decided to take one last dive into the theological deep end. "Craig, I love your honesty. Here's how I see it. Thoughtful Christians know that in the past we've read the Bible wrong about slav-

> "Our research shows that one-third of gays and lesbians attend church regularly, across a wide spectrum of denominations and backgrounds, including Catholic, mainline, nonmainline, and nondenominational churches. Most gays and lesbians in America align themselves with Christianity, and one-sixth have beliefs that qualify them as born-again Christians."
>
> Kinnaman and Lyons,
> *unChristian*, 97–98

ery, the cosmos, and the treatment of women. But if I may also keep it real, many of those same thoughtful Christians are not able to embrace the argument for homosexuality and say, 'Okay, homosexuality is just fine!'"[2]

I noticed the restaurant staff standing off to the side, waiting for us to surrender our table.

"We have really worn out our welcome, you guys; we need to wrap this up. It's almost 1:00 a.m. and we have another day of this conference in front of us." We left a seriously large tip for our waitress, and we all agreed we needed to be a kinder, gentler version of ourselves with her the next night. We headed for the door and Craig headed to his room.

"I've got to do some more editing on the interviews, you guys."

"Tonight?" I shot back incredulously.

"Sure," Craig responded, "we need to have some of them ready for the morning events."

"Well, I don't know about you, Jim," Todd said, "but this old guy needs to hit the hay." Todd, who spends a great deal of time on the road, is not what you'd call a late night party animal.

Craig got on the elevator, and I asked Todd to sit in the lobby and give me a couple more minutes. The place was as quiet as a mortuary. Todd really wanted to get to his room, but being the most "otherly" person on our team, he agreed to a few more minutes.

"Todd, you and I are both dads. We have adult and young adult kids. I like how one preacher put it: 'When I was young I had five theories and no kids; now I have five kids and no theories.' So on a personal level, how does all this play out for you and Debbie and your kids?"

"Jim, I know there's been a lot of talk in the last ten years about postmodernism and the loss of absolute truth. I know the church seems very worried about it. And I am sure that there are real threats to the gospel in the postmodern world—as there were in the modern and pre-modern worlds. But I actually think something bigger is going on: post-Christendom.

"Here's why. Postmodernism is above the heads of most of us. But the rejection of Christians by current culture hits us in the gut. It hurts! It puts us off! Ironically, outsiders feel put off by us as well. Add those two realities together and you get this: while evangelistic conversations have never been easy, today they are worse than your first junior high dance—if that's possible.

"Okay, I'm done. I have to get some sleep so I can keep up with your slave-driving ways tomorrow morning."

And then, like all great preachers, he offered one closing story.

"Here's what I suggest. There is one thing everyone who fishes knows: you catch fish on their terms, not yours! If the fish are eating at 5:00 a.m. and you roll out of bed and head for the lake at the crack of 11:00 a.m., guess who is catching zero fish? If the fish are all on the south side of the lake but you insist on fishing on the north side—again, guess who is going home with zero fish?

"Jesus said, 'Come follow me and I'll make you fishers of men.' This is a big challenge for much of the church. Why? Because we value our traditions so much, we confuse change with compromise. 'We can't go to other side of the lake,' we think, 'we've always fished on this side.' We rationalize, saying, 'This is where grandma's house is; we've always fished

114

under that big oak tree, sitting on an old stump.' But now, for whatever reason, all the fish have moved to the north end of the lake.

"What do we do now? Do we stand on the shore and curse the fish? 'You damn fish! How dare you become postmodern, post-Christian, sexually confused and tolerant fish?' While that's tempting, there is a better way. Go to granny's garage, get the canoe down from the rafters, hose it off, find the paddles, and go to where the fish are—meeting them on their terms.

"This is not easy. We will fail a lot! We will even inadvertently compromise or offend people. If we commit to diversity and difference, there is no risk-free ground to stand on.

"This time we'll have to follow Jesus and walk on water."

GETTING PAST GAY

Climbing the Mountain of Difference with Dad

Craig Spinks

"I'm afraid I'm not going to say what you want me to say, Craig."

Even over the phone I could tell my dad was concerned about his visit to Colorado. I'd invited him out so that we could have some face-to-face conversations as part of my research for *The Outsider Interviews*. His visit was just a few days away, and the realities were starting to kick in.

"Here's the deal, Dad: I'm not looking for you to say anything. I just want the two of us to explore what it might look like to talk about faith, especially the parts we disagree about. I guess I'm intrigued to see if we could do that without it turning into an argument."

I'd never really seen my dad nervous like this before. I can only imagine that it'd be pretty intimidating to have your son initiate a conversation about getting along better.

Then my dad popped *the* question: "Are you going to make me talk about homosexuality?"

Looking Back

I was raised in southwest Ohio in an evangelical Christian home. My parents divorced when I was eleven, and shortly thereafter my brother and I chose to live with my dad, who was and still is deeply committed to his traditional faith. Living in a testosterone-filled household provided plenty of opportunities to see my dad in good times and in bad. But somehow he managed to model Christianity in a positive light. Ultimately, he is the reason I became a Christ-follower. He was always challenging me to think about life as it related to faith and talked openly about his own beliefs. This was all in addition to making sure we were active in our church.

Our relationship started to change after I turned twenty and began asking questions about my faith. I realized that most of what I believed was based on things I had been taught, and I wasn't sure if I really owned those beliefs for myself. I started a process I now call "recycling my faith," where I pressed the reset button and started over. I kept some beliefs and discarded others, but I primarily reshaped the things I'd been taught to better reflect my personal experience with God. I call this recycling because I didn't just discard the faith I grew up with; rather I reused and redeemed parts of it so that it could be useful in my life today. I began to trust myself and Jesus a little more and what I'd been taught a little less.

Naturally, some of my beliefs started to diverge from my dad's. When these new differences arose, I spoke up and defended my position. We both cared a lot about our respective positions, so it seemed that the more transparent I was, the more we argued. After a year or two and a number of painful arguments, I started to question the benefit of talking with my dad about these issues. When it came to things we were likely to disagree about, maybe we all would be better off if I kept my mouth shut—which is ultimately what I did. When he'd bring up something I disagreed with, I'd bite my tongue and keep quiet. The arguing stopped, but so did our conversations about faith.

Well, not entirely. We still have spiritual conversations, but they are usually about stuff we know we'll agree on and actually not very relevant to my current spiritual journey. Even when safe opportunities present themselves, I find myself steering us away from anything close to my heart. I guess I'm afraid of being hurt. Not that my dad has ever directly tried to hurt me with his words, but when we argue I usually end up feeling hurt in some way. I'm like most people, I suppose. The closer the topic is to my heart, the more it hurts when the conversation turns into a fight.

A Hopeful Sign

When my dad asked if I would make him talk about homosexuality, I thought, *Oh boy, what am I getting myself into?*

"Yeah, that's a possibility," I responded. "But I don't see us coming to any conclusions about that topic. I just want to explore whether it's possible for us to talk about something like homosexuality without it resulting in an anger-filled, intellectual debate."

Dad moved on. "I watched your video of Rio the other night."

See the video Craig sent to his dad before his visit.
Watch the clip "Rio's Story."

In preparation for our conversations I'd given Dad a few assignments that included reading David Kinnaman's and Gabe Lyons's *unChristian* and watching a short clip from my one-on-one interview with Rio in Denver. I was interested to see how my dad would respond to Rio talking about her struggle with homosexuality.

"Well, Craig, I have to admit, I've never heard a homosexual talk about how they've struggled with the idea of being gay, let alone talk about ways they've tried to stop. In most interviews I've seen with gays, they seem hyper-sure of themselves. It feels to me as if they want to shove their lifestyle in our faces by parading their relationships and complaining about not having equal rights."

It seemed that Rio's transparency, vulnerability, and humility had earned some points with Dad. He understood that Rio currently considers herself gay, but it mattered to him that at one time she didn't want that for herself and tried to avoid it. I exhaled a sigh of relief, encouraged by my dad's ability to listen to Rio. Maybe it would be possible for us to have a civil conversation despite our differences. Still a little gun-shy, I told dad that we'd talk more about this when he was in town. After a few more minutes talking about the rest of the family, we wrapped up the conversation.

My hope for *The Outsider Interviews* has always been that it would help parents like my dad better understand their kids. In many ways our relationship captures the dilemma more and more Christian parents are experiencing with their adult children. What better way to try to overcome our differences than for my dad and me to have a real conversation? My dad's visit seemed like a great idea a couple months ago, but it turns out, the idea of dialogue is easier in theory than in practice. Each conversation I had with my dad about this project brought an overwhelming feeling of anxiety—fear of rejection and shame. I vacillated between being hopeful and hopeless. I had been hopeless, so our phone conversation brought some well-needed confidence in my dad's upcoming trip.

Missing Dad

I had been missing my dad's involvement in my spiritual life—not the arguments and debates but the everyday conversations we had in my teenage years. I'm able to have these conversations with other people; why can't I have them with my dad? While this project is not the most natural approach, it has allowed us to be very intentional about reclaiming this aspect of our relationship, and that was the reason for my dad's visit to Colorado.

As my wife Sara and I prepared for his visit, we contemplated whether to stash some things out of sight—half-empty bottles of liquor; our DVD collection, which includes a number of controversial films; and books that he would think contained questionable theological viewpoints. I used to be more cautious about what was within sight around my dad, but this time it was different. I wanted to let my dad see the version of me who is alive with passion instead of the candy-coated version I sometimes present. A part of that "real me" is in the movies I watch, the books I read, and the people I have drinks with.

What was I afraid of losing? Respect, for starters. In all honesty, I'm a "words of affirmation" junkie. I've consistently had people in my life who have been incredibly affirming and encouraging. Without them I don't know where I'd be. My dad is my number one fan, always rooting from the sidelines. In my darkest hours he's been at my side. Perhaps that's why it hurts so much when we disagree. Maybe I feel like his affirmation is sometimes conditional. It's not that I think we should always agree. I just want to feel as though he accepts me even if he disagrees with me.

Tense Dinner Conversation

My dad's flight arrived an hour late due to bad weather. This was ironic because I take every chance I get to rub in Colorado's great weather with my dad, who still lives in Cincinnati. Since he would be in town for just a couple of days, I had a short window of time to prove Colorado's beauty, and, well, we weren't off to a good start.

He got the first shot in. "Great weather, Craig."

"Yeah, we shipped it in especially for you," I said as we hugged and then headed for baggage claim.

We caught up while driving from the airport to downtown Denver. Sara was along for the ride and would be joining us for the weekend's activities. It was comforting to have her there not just for her perspective in our conversations but also because I knew Dad and I would be on our best behavior with her in the room.

Dad was buying us dinner that night (an offer we never refuse) and had picked a restaurant he remembered from a childhood trip to Denver. As soon as I walked through the doors I understood why he liked this place. Every square inch of wall space was filled with mounted heads of elk, deer, bear, and bison. My dad, an avid hunter, must have felt like he was at Disneyland. I couldn't help but think that if I ever have a cruel desire to torture my vegetarian friends, this is where I'll bring them. We all ordered steak.

As I ate, my jaw started to clench. Each bite brought more nervousness. At some point we needed to get down to business, and I wasn't sure how to make that happen without it feeling unnatural. Luckily, I can always count on Dad to bring up controversial topics. I don't know if he does it because he's unabashedly honest or if he likes getting a rise out of me, but tonight I was grateful for his brashness, whatever the motive. "Craig, I hate to be a downer, but I just don't see things getting any better for America. With this recession and the moral decline, I just see us heading on the same path as Rome."

"Seriously?" It took me a couple minutes to wrap my head around what my dad was saying. "So are you saying that you think that America is less moral today than it was in the sixties and seventies?"

"Absolutely. If someone were to have told me in the seventies that Americans, even some Christians, would be accepting of homosexuality and abortion, I wouldn't have believed it."

As Dad continued to make his point, I began to realize that he and I have very different ideas of what morality looks like.[1] In his mind the acceptance of homosexuality is a clear indication of moral decline, while I think being more loving and accepting of the gay community is a sign of less hatred and judgment. Dad sees the world crumbling down; I see it improving.

Remembering my commitment to keeping it real, I responded, "I actually see a lot of hope in our world today. I see young people wanting to make the world a better place. I see the world becoming smaller and working together with a little more unity and young Christians becoming spiritually awakened rather than blindly adhering to religion."

Dad was glad to hear that people my age are optimistic, but he couldn't share my enthusiasm. After politely listening, he continued to tick off the signs of moral decline and inevitable destruction of the earth. I felt like he was channeling Pat Robertson, Hal Lindsey, and James Dobson all at once. I wanted to share about how I see the return of Jesus as being less about the earth's destruction and more about restoring earth to its original intent, but the more my dad talked, the angrier I got. This wasn't heading where I wanted it to. We were falling back into our old patterns. My dad didn't seem to be very interested in my point of view, and I was bottling up anger and about to explode. But before I could say something I'd later regret, we were saved by jetlag catching up with my dad. We left a tip and headed home to get a good night's rest.

Picking Our Way through Rocks and Boulders

Things looked better the next morning. It was sixty degrees and sunny outside, and I didn't have to start the day apologizing for something I said the night before. Maybe a new day would bring new understanding between us. "I'm glad you'll get to experience some real Colorado weather while you're here!" I said, ribbing him.

"Yeah, yeah. What do you think I should wear on our hike?"

My dad introduced my brother and me to hiking growing up. While other families were going to the beach, we were hiking to the bottom of the Grand Canyon. In my adult years that has transitioned into yearly mountain climbing expeditions as a family. We've bagged a number of state high points, including Rainier in Washington, Hood in Oregon, Whitney in California, and the list goes on. These trips have been where my Dad and I have had our best and worst moments.

Thirty minutes later dad, Sara, and I were hiking in the foothills of Boulder County. After the previous night's challenges I was reluctant to start up the conversation, but Dad kicked it off nicely. "Craig, the other day on the phone you asked me to think of some questions for you." He pulled a piece of paper out of his pocket and carefully unfolded it. I was nervous but glad he had taken the time to think through some questions. He continued, "Okay, here's my first question: Why do you have such a problem with church?"

For some reason this question made me realize that most of our conversations of late have been focused on hot-button issues, and we've never really talked broadly about my journey of recycling my faith, so I took this opportunity to share a bit of that with him. It was a long answer to a simple question, but I eventually got back on track. "I don't have a problem with church, nor do I think it is a waste of time, but the traditional expressions of church just don't work for me the way they used to. The benefits of going to church I see are for connection with a community of Christians as well as having regular encouragement in spiritual growth. While many people find this in the context of a church, I've found it elsewhere in settings that are more natural for me."

Dad had more questions. It felt good having him take the initiative—less complicated. "Okay, so what else have you recycled, Craig?"

"Frankly, Dad, a lot of my beliefs and practices are being reshaped. For example, you taught me methods for how to pray, and through those methods I began to experience what I call communion with God. I think being in communion with God is what prayer is all about. Along the way I started to notice that I was also finding communion with God in ways I wasn't taught, for instance while hiking or listening to music. Since these methods are more natural for me, I've ended up counting that as prayer and not relying on the traditional methods as much."

"Does that mean that you think structure and tradition are pointless?" he asked with a slight tinge of disappointment.

"Not at all! That structure and tradition helped me get to where I am today, but at times I feel the structure gets valued more than what the structure holds up. For instance, I feel like the act of praying is valued more than the connection with God that happens when you pray. I've seen people in the church who are more concerned about upholding the structures of religion than having a relationship with our Creator. If I were to have a problem with church, that would be it."

The conversation came to a natural break as we pulled out our water bottles and trail mix and enjoyed the scenery for a few minutes. But since I was on a mission, not just a hike, I took the initiative and started the conversation back up, referring to my brother's perspective.

"Hey, Dad, when I told Dan about this project, he said it was pointless for the two of us to talk about things we disagree on. The way he sees it, you just want to change me, and I just want to change you. What do you think about that?"

After a brief pause he replied, "Well, yeah, up until the point when you became an adult, it was my job to shape you into a good Christian. I felt such a relief after you moved out because I didn't have that pressure anymore. It's your responsibility now."

While I would have objected at age seventeen or eighteen, what my dad said actually made some sense to me. In my teenage years I was independent and resistant to my dad imposing values on me, but as the prospect of having my own kids draws closer, I'm now wondering how Sara and I will handle this. I'm sure Dad would prefer I'd think and act more like him today, but from what he was saying, he no longer felt a pressure or duty to change me. I, on the other hand, had recently realized that I had not let my dad go. I realized that I had some confessing of my own to do.

"Dad, I've thought a lot about what Dan said, and I think he was right about me. I do want to change you. It's funny—I can talk with all kinds of people with whom I disagree, not caring whether or not we ultimately agree. But when it comes to you, I guess I care a little more. I really don't want to be the kind of person who imposes his beliefs on others, so I'm going to try really hard to respect your opinions more and to not try to change them.

"While I'm at it, I've wanted to talk with you about a few other things. I've made some assumptions about what you believe and have embraced stereotypes rather than really trying to understand you. I'm sorry; you deserve better than that. I've also said and done some things purely to get a rise out of you."

"You mean like the time you used the f-word?" Dad was recalling a situation a few years back when some bottled-up anger got released in the form of profanity.

"Yeah, that's a good example. The only reason I said that was really just to tick you off. Again, I'm sorry about that, but it exposes a deeper issue. A lot of times I'll avoid talking about something controversial with you until the point when I explode. When that happens I feel like an idiot because not only do I treat you poorly, but I also misrepresent the thing that originally upset me. I really want to learn how to open up before exploding, but I need something in return, Dad. I need to know that even though you and I may disagree, you will always accept me."

Dad looked me in the eye. "Craig, I am so proud of you. Nothing you could say or do would ever keep me from accepting you. You need to know that."

An awkward sense of closeness settled over the two of us. *So this is what it's supposed to feel like*, I remember thinking. We picked our way through the rocks and small boulders as we made our way back to the car in silence. On the drive back home, we picked up a pizza at a local favorite, Beau Jo's Pizza, and brought it home with us.

Failing Bridges

As the three of us were busy canceling out the calories burned on the hike, I walked over to the TV and put a copy of

The Outsider Interviews into the DVD player. The hike was completed, but my mission wasn't. One of the reasons behind my desire for peaceful conversations is that I'd like to be able to include my dad in the things I'm most passionate about. Currently those passions overlap a lot with the things we disagree about. Many of the views presented in *The Outsider Interviews* fit into this category, so I thought watching a few clips would be a good way to see if we were any closer to communicating better. I started with the main segment from Kansas City. As Klarisa and Sarah recounted their bad experiences with Christians, my Dad grabbed the remote and pressed the pause button multiple times, the way people who are anxious repeatedly push the walk button at a crosswalk.

"That's not fair, Craig. Christians are overwhelmingly kind and loving, and all these people are talking about is their bad experiences. Surely the evangelism experiences they are talking about are with wackos. I know many people who came to faith because of the Four Spiritual Laws."

"How old are those people, Dad?"

"Forties, fifties. Why?"

I pulled out my laptop and clicked on a photo of the "Bridge to Nowhere" that Todd and Jim use to illustrate how things have changed. "Dad, this is a real photo of a bridge that at one point in time was extremely useful; it helped people cross a river. But a hurricane came through and changed the course of the river so that now it no longer flows under the bridge. The bridge is no longer useful. That bridge is like our evangelism methods; they were useful at one point in time, but the river has moved."

129

Sara chimed in. "Christians *are* loving, but every single one of my coworkers has talked to me at one time or another about their bad experiences with Christians or the church. And when I used the Four Spiritual Laws in college with the college ministry I was a part of, people just weren't receptive. They hated it. And so did I!"

"How old are your coworkers, Sara?" Dad asked.

"Mostly Craig's and my age—late twenties."

I added, "People tend to remember bad experiences more than positive ones. So even though a lot of positive things are happening in Christianity, that's not what we are known for. What we learned from the book *unChristian* is that Christianity has an overwhelmingly negative reputation among outsiders."

I could tell that something was starting to click for my dad as he responded. "They showed a video clip at church a while back asking people what they thought of Christianity and comparing that to what they thought of Jesus. People responded negatively to Christianity, but positively to Jesus."

"Yeah, there are even books out about that phenomenon," I replied.[2] "But let's keep rolling through these clips, Dad. We've got to head for the airport pretty soon."

We finished up Kansas City and moved to Denver. I didn't plan to save talking about homosexuality until the end of Dad's trip, but that's what ended up happening. The clip I'd sent before Dad's visit was of Rio's interview offstage with me; we were now watching the main interview, which triggered some new thoughts for Dad.

Just a few seconds into the segment where Rio comes out about her homosexuality, Dad was once again attacking the defenseless pause button. "It's absolutely absurd for her to use the words *Christian* and *gay* in the same sentence. The Bible is absolutely clear that homosexuality is wrong."

"So you don't think that someone who is gay can be a Christian?"

"Absolutely not, just like I don't think someone who is addicted to drugs can be a Christian."

"Really?" I was surprised by Dad's certainty.

"Yeah, if someone embraces behavior that is sinful, I don't think that person has really dedicated their life to Christ. They are choosing a lifestyle of sin over a Christian lifestyle. You can't have it both ways."

"But using your example," Sara chimed in, "it's often hard or even impossible for someone to stop using drugs."

"True, but Christians with a drug problem acknowledge that drug use is bad and are trying to stop, whereas the gay community isn't trying to get better. They say that it isn't a sin even though the Bible clearly says it is. That's the difference for me. If someone who is addicted to drugs was saying that drug use is okay and that they're a Christian, I'd say the same thing—they're not."

I get a little sensitive when it comes to people defining who's in and who's out; my tone began to reflect this. "But Dad, many homosexuals don't read those verses the same way as you. Do you think those in the gay community who call themselves Christians really believe that it's *not a sin*, or do you think it's just a cover-up?"

"Oh, I think they believe they're not sinning, but they're wrong. Craig, this is one topic we are never going to see eye to eye on."

That was one thing we could agree about. No matter how much we talked about this, not much was going to change in our interaction on the homosexuality issue. Mercifully, it was time for us to head for the airport.

As we pulled up to the airport and said our good-byes, I wanted to try one more time to get my dad to understand, but I knew that would have to wait for another day. We parted like two respectful, and perhaps wiser sparring partners.

On the Way Home

As Sara and I headed back home, she asked me to remind her why I wanted to be able to talk to my dad about these things. "It's not so much that I want to talk with my dad about homosexuality," I said. "I just want to be able to talk about tough topics as they come up rather than avoiding them. I like hearing his viewpoints. They challenge my thinking. That's really what's behind this whole attempt to connect with him."

After gazing out the window for couple of minutes, Sara circled back. "I guess I understand wanting to hear different perspectives, but why do you want this from your dad, of all people?"

"I've thought about that a lot, and honestly I'm not really sure. Maybe I'm just looking for his approval. But deep down I feel like our relationship has been disconnected the past couple years, and I think that learning how to navigate our differences will ultimately improve our relationship as a whole."

"But what are you looking for from your dad? What do you need from him?"

"Well, for starters I need to feel like he's not dismissing my views simply because they are different from his. I need to know that he loves me and doesn't judge me—I need him to tell me not just with his words but also with his actions. It felt amazing today when he told me that he accepted me no matter what. Now I just need his actions to communicate this. A huge piece of this for me is listening. I just want him to listen to my perspectives and maybe even show some curiosity about my viewpoint before jumping to his counterarguments."

My wife was on a mission to get to the bottom of what motivated me.

"Craig, if you were to put yourself in your dad's shoes, what would you have done differently? More to the point, what do you think we should do differently when we have kids ourselves?"

"Well, I don't think my dad did such a bad job. I hope I haven't been too hard on him. Let's face it, the question isn't *if* we're going to screw up our kids, it's *how*! But one thing I do think we should do differently is to teach our kids how to explore faith rather than adopt a set of beliefs. I want to help them process through why something is good or bad so they own the choice themselves. I wonder how my conversations with my dad might be different today if, for instance, instead of telling me all the reasons why homosexuality is bad, he asked me about why I wrestle with the issue. That way he'd be joining me in a journey rather than trying to be the tour guide."

As Sara and I drove westward toward the beautiful Rockies, we talked about ways we might approach parenting some-day—a topic we find both scary and exciting.

I'd love to end by saying my dad and I now have a perfect relationship, but that wouldn't be true. I'm sure my dad and I will continue to get into arguments and say things we regret, but I also think we have taken some steps in the right direction.

At some point in the not-too-distant future, the rubber will hit the road. A conversation will arise that's not part of a research project, and a referee might not be in the room. Since I've now resigned from trying to change my dad, the only person I have left to work on is me! The real issue isn't my dad's communication skills but whether I will be able to be more respectful of his views. Will we communicate acceptance despite our differences? Or will we fall back into our well-traveled ruts of difference? I may be naïve, but I have hope my dad and I will continue to forge a new relationship marked by mutual respect and acceptance.

Time will tell.

SEATTLE OUTSIDERS

The Great Agreement

Jim Henderson

> This chapter correlates with the video titled
> **"The Great Agreement"**
> in the Seattle section of your DVD.

Don't invite me to church—invite me to serve.

Audrey

We presented our final Outsider Interview in Seattle, home of some of the most innovative companies in America. Microsoft, Eddie Bauer, Starbucks, Boeing, Amazon, Real Networks, and The EMP (The Experience Music Project) all call Seattle home.

Off The Map, one of the organizations I lead, has hosted an annual conference in Seattle every year since 2001. We've built up a fairly strong following as well as a significant team of volunteers who help us "put on the show." We conducted the final interview on the second day of the conference. It was great to have our team and all the musicians we've worked with over the years on site. Most people say they've never been to an event quite like Off The Map. We describe it as being more like a concert and less like a conference.

Calvary, a historic Assembly of God church, hosted this Outsider Interview. Forty years ago this was one of the most revolutionary churches in Seattle. They had a great deal of influence on me as a young Christian, so it was something like a homecoming for me. I was anxious to return the blessing this church had once bestowed on me.

On this Outsider Interviews tour we worked with Anglican, missional/emerging, Lutheran, and now Assembly of God churches. This denominational mix keeps people guessing, which we like.

As was mentioned earlier, for our money the most significant thing Kinnaman and Lyons discovered wasn't the difference between outsiders and insiders but rather the startling similarities these groups share, which may help explain why regardless of the issue we raised, we couldn't get our guests in Seattle to disagree about anything. That's why instead of "The Great Debate," we called this chapter "The Great Agreement."

Recruiters "R" Us

Finding a couple of non-Christians who are willing to be called *outsiders* and get on stage in a roomful of what they fear will be rabid evangelicals can be quite the adventure.

People who take on the job of recruiting are impacted profoundly themselves.

Jeff Smith was one of our recruiters.

Jeff is a math coach and grad student at Seattle University.
Jeff decided to ask Audrey, a fellow student, if she might be
interested in being a guest on our show.

Jeff approached Audrey a couple of weeks before the show
to see if she would enjoy telling the truth to a roomful of
Christians.

"Sure, Jeff, what do they want me to say?"

"They just want you to give your opinion about Christians
and Christianity."

"Jeff, I'm not a Christian."

"Exactly, Audrey. That's why they're asking for your opinion. They want to know how the people they're trying to
connect with feel about Christianity."

"You mean they want me to tell them what I actually think,
Jeff, like a focus group?"

"You got it. Plus they'll throw in dinner and $50."

"Where do I sign?"

Audrey was tentative, but she'd learned to trust Jeff.

Because I'm from Seattle I have a lot of friends here. I
asked them to help me find some interesting insiders and
outsiders for this interview.

Steve Lewis is one of those people. Steve is very connected
with both insiders and outsiders. He leads The Purple Door,
a kind of Christian rooming house situated right across the
street from the University of Washington. That's where we
found Charlie. Charlie is an incredibly bright atheist. He not
only hangs out with Steve, he actually rents a room from him.
The night of the interview a pewful of Christian students

showed up to cheer Charlie on as he attempted to help Christians understand things from his point of view.

That's how we found our two outsiders, but how about the insiders? Where did they come from?

Finding Christians who "get" what we're trying to do in the Outsider Interviews can be tricky. For some reason as Christians age, they seem to get less playful, which is one reason we prefer to work with young people. We also use a lot of self-deprecating humor, which Christians sometimes confuse with mockery. The fact is, we're just trying to help Christians see themselves through the eyes of outsiders—the same group they talk about reaching out to every Sunday.

Would you believe that one of our guests is an international jump rope champion? Chandra talks about it in this clip. **Watch the clip "Jump Rope for Jesus."**

Elizabeth Chapin began volunteering for Off The Map events several years ago. I asked her to help us find a young insider who had opinions but wasn't *mean*. Elizabeth had gone to church with a young woman named Chandra at Overlake Christian, a megachurch across the lake from Seattle. Chandra jumped at the chance and agreed to be a guest on our show. (Besides being a heartfelt follower of Jesus, Chandra is an international jump rope champion. No lie.)

My last call was to Jim Caldwell, one of the regional directors for Young Life in the Seattle area. Jim and I are not what you would call close friends, but we hang out with many of the same people, which is almost a better way of getting to know someone. Jim is one of those guys I would want to have on my side if I had to be in a street fight. He has "I've got your back" written all over him.

Unfortunately, a couple insiders we had lined up to do the interview dropped out at the last minute, so I called Jim the day of and asked if he knew anyone who could get onstage without any prep. He told me he had just the guy. His name was Matt.

Matt was raised in Texas but had obviously spent a lot of time in Seattle. Wearing a knit cap, khakis, and sandals, he could have been confused with a member of Pearl Jam. His "Beyond Malibu" T-shirt didn't do much to cover up his affiliation with Young Life, which he described in a typical Seattle way as a local nonprofit.

After getting our guests situated onstage and properly introduced to the Seattle audience, we dove right into the deep end and asked if they thought Christianity had gotten too cozy with politics. The outsiders said what you would expect, but not the insiders—they didn't spend one minute defending Christianity's involvement in politics.

> "Three-quarters of young outsiders and half of young churchgoers describe present-day Christianity as 'too involved in politics.' Nearly two-thirds of Mosaic and Buster outsiders and nearly half of young born-again Christians said they perceive 'the political efforts of conservative Christians' to be a problem facing America."
>
> Kinnaman and Lyons, *unChristian*, 155

Charlie captured their sentiments best: "Christianity is a *brand* that has become associated with one particular political party."

I wondered how a word like *politics* that was once anathema to Christians had evolved into part of our religious vocabulary. In the past thirty years, being a Christian politician had become a *calling* and evangelicalism's influence had reached the highest office in the land. In many ways we'd won—or had we?

139

Politics had come up in some of our other interviews, but in Seattle it was front and center. I was anxious to unpack this topic with Todd and Craig after the show.

The topic of politics came up in our Phoenix interview as well. Erin offers, "I've never met a Christian who wasn't a Republican."

Watch the clip "Republican Christian Oxymoron?"

Our guests surprised us with their opinions on issues from the veracity of the Bible to the philosophical construct known as *certainty*. I was certain of one thing: the sensitive topics and virtual lovefest of viewpoints was causing some of the older saints in the audience concern. Most of them had committed to memory "come out from among them, and be ye separate" (2 Cor. 6:17 KJV) by the age of six.

I signaled the house band for help.

They caught my drift and brought Jessica Ketola onstage.

With her usual flair, Jessica proceeded to rock the house with "I Need to Wake Up."[1] Pretty soon everyone was singing—young, old, insiders, outsiders—all caught up in an anthem of change. I secretly wondered how many people knew that Melissa Etheridge, an openly gay woman, had composed this song.

Our Last Stop

Coffeehouses are to Seattle what churches are to Nashville. I tell you without exaggeration that on many street corners you can find *two* Starbucks coffee shops plus a nearby Larry's Late Nite Latte, where you can get your caffeine delivered to your car at midnight. My favorite hangout is a bookstore/coffeehouse/food court called Third Place Books. This is one of many locations where I "office" in Seattle. I knew they would be open 'til nine that night so we could grab a bite after the show and get started on our after-the-interview write-a-thon.

"Jim, Todd, I've got the car waiting—let's go." Craig loves Seattle and wanted to see what he could fit in while it was still light out. We wrapped up the event around four, said our good-byes, jumped in the rental, and headed for Third Place.

Craig was driving, but he caught Todd's eye in the rearview mirror. "Could you believe how much that group agreed with each other, Todd?"

"I think that's our story, Craig. I know it's a different twist, but it really did reflect just how similar young insiders and outsiders are in their viewpoints. Remember I was telling you about my daughter Carolyn? She is a believer, but she probably hangs out with outsiders more than insiders."

"In two hundred feet, *bear left*." Craig doesn't travel anywhere without his GPS, which for fun was set to speak in a British accent.

I spotted Third Place. "There it is, Craig—follow that yellow VW."

We walked in to find teriyaki, scones, pizza, BBQ, thousands of books, hundreds of people, and coffee—lots and lots of coffee. Laptops dominated the jumbo, pine-top tables, kids were running around, and a three-piece bluegrass group was playing something from *O Brother, Where Art Thou?* I love this place.

Being a regular at Third Place, I knew where to find one of the highly coveted electrical outlets. The three of us plugged in and I stood guard. While our laptops rushed to catch up with us, Craig headed for Big Time Pizza and Todd for Burney Brothers BBQ.

By the time the guys got back to the table, I was up to my ears in bluegrass.

Todd jolted me back to reality. "Jim, check out these ribs!"

"Burney Brothers, Todd—only the best for the new priest."

"Right. Hey, speaking of which, Jim, I think you could use a good confession."

Craig slid his pizza in front of us and invited us to dig into the pepperoni, sausage, and banana pepper special.

We washed down the pizza and ribs with beer, iced tea, and Diet Coke and laughed out loud as we reminisced about the places we'd visited. We talked about the outsiders to whom we'd become attached. This project has been a load of fun, but we had one more show to get on paper.

I got the conversation started as Todd and Craig completed the membership requirements of the clean plate club. They were still chewing, but now their eyes were on me. I swung my chair away from the bluegrass toward Todd and Craig. "Let's talk about politics."

They gulped down their final bites.

"I had a pretty liberal upbringing," I started, "but after I got saved, liberal equaled evil. Conversely, I gave conservative Christians a pass on almost everything. When I was planting my first church in 1977, I had no idea that my ministry life was converging with a new political movement called the Moral Majority. Being a sucker for anything revolutionary, I spent the better part of that year taking a close look at the religious right. As it turned out (fortunately for me), I was too preoccupied preaching the evacuation gospel to bother with earthly politics, so I never got involved, but I never dreamed of voting for a *liberal* Democrat.

"How about you, Todd? You grew up in Orange County, a hotbed of conservatism. How did that mix with your Christianity?"

"The truth, Jim?" Todd asked hesitantly.

"Lay it on me."

"To be honest, it never crossed my mind that Christians could be Democrats. Well, there was that Democrat Jimmy Carter in my high school years, but boy did that presidency get a bad rap!

> "Among the evangelical segment, only a slight majority are registered Republicans (59 percent). That's a high proportion, but far removed from the monolithic levels one might expect based on media pronouncements or the expectations of Christian leaders. We are projecting, for instance, that in the 2008 election, as many born-again Christians (including both evangelicals and nonevangelicals) will cast a ballot as registered Democrats as will vote as Republicans. Party affiliation does not always translate directly to candidate choice, but it is a reminder that the Christian community is more diverse, less cohesive, and less unified than is typically assumed."
>
> Kinnaman and Lyons, *unChristian*, 160

"Anyway, I found myself agreeing with our guests about Christians' over-involvement in politics. Sadly, it's become a foregone conclusion that the right wing *is* the Christian wing. Maybe it's my age, but these days I see both wings as correct on some things and wrong on others. For me, no political party represents the Jesus way, the way of the kingdom of God."

Kids were running under our table and making a racket, but it was fun to be in a room with so much energy.

Politics came up in Denver as well. Andrew articulates the dilemma of how good intentions don't always translate into good actions. **Watch the clip "Christians Being Played."**

"This is a topic that outsiders *and* insiders seemed to agree on in almost every city we visited," I said. "The church has simply gotten way too far in bed with power. I remember you saying something about the church being its most productive when we're operating on the margins. Based on what these young people are telling us, we've wandered too close to the center."

Craig was disinterested in all the political talk. He waited patiently while Todd and I reminisced, but he had something else on his mind. "The same way it bugs you guys that the church has gotten in bed with politics, it bugs me that Christians come across like a bunch of know-it-alls."

"Sounds like the swagger problem we were talking about in Kansas City," I replied.

"Probably just another way of saying the same thing, but here's what I mean. Do you guys remember how Audrey responded to the question about her religious status? She said that she wasn't very certain about anything. And you know what? I really identified with her. You'd think that after twenty-eight years of being a Christian, I'd be more certain, but actually the reverse is true. I feel like I was given a few puzzle pieces twenty-eight years ago but no box with a picture of the finished product on the cover. I look at those pieces and become more certain of what I think the puzzle is supposed to look like, but in actuality I really don't know for sure. I'm basing my confidence solely on the few pieces in my hand. As I've grown and listened to others like Audrey, I've become more aware that other puzzle pieces exist, which humbles me. This doesn't mean I'm not certain about how God works in my life; it just means I'm aware that there is more to the puzzle than I can see, which in turn makes me less likely to proclaim certainty. Apparently this scenario makes many

Craig's not alone. Matt, Sarah, and Alex are insiders who are not as certain as many of their fellow insiders would like them to be. **Watch the clip "Bottom Line Beliefs."**

Christians nervous, while for me it has the opposite effect—it actually increases my faith. If I had access to the big picture and knew where all of the pieces fit, in my opinion I wouldn't need faith."

Todd leaned in. "That was beautifully put, Craig, but I do have some pushback for you. It's one thing to say *I don't know for certain* about this or that. But it is another thing altogether to say *it is impossible to know anything for certain*. I think Christians can admit to lots of uncertainty as long as we are on the road to pursuing as much truth as we can—and doing it not just to be right but to love and humbly serve others. As I see it, uncertainty is completely contextual. Neurotic dodging of the truth, for example, in order to live in all manner of harmful behavior is not good for anyone. But honest seeking, which temporarily increases a sense of uncertainty, is not only a good and normal thing, it's the basis for beautiful conversations about faith."

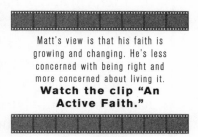

Matt's view is that his faith is growing and changing. He's less concerned with being right and more concerned about living it. **Watch the clip "An Active Faith."**

I heard my name being called in the distance. Some friends from the conference had followed us to Third Place Books.

"How did you guys know we would be here?" I asked.

"Jim, there are only three or four places you hang out— Vivace's, Ladros, and Third Place Books. How hard could it be? The other two places close early, so we headed here."

I was embarrassed to be so predictable.

"Grab a coffee, you guys. We're collecting our thoughts about the Outsider Interview. We need to hear how you thought it went."

As they wandered off to locate some caffeine, we wandered back into *the uncertainty of certainty*. I had lots of feelings about this topic, so I decided to put them squarely on the table.

"Todd, I agree with Craig. I think Christianity has become way too certain of itself. Couple that with political involvement and public exposure, and you get swagger. We've exchanged faith for certainty. Actually I welcome Audrey and Craig's critique, and I hope it pushes us back where we belong, which is in the faith business."

"I agree with you and Craig," Todd added. "Something has gone terribly wrong with the way outsiders experience faith and certainty, but I think what we need is a humble mix of faith and knowledge based on love for others. That might be a good way forward."

Our table was already buried in laptops, food trays, and half-empty plates, but our friends found room for their coffee and cookies and squeezed in. We were anxious to hear what they thought about the interview. We peppered them with questions.

"So what did you guys think?" I asked.

"Which of our guests made the biggest impression on you?" Craig added.

"What surprised you the most?" Todd blurted.

"Whoa, slow down. What are you guys doing, writing a book or something?" Our good friend Rose was trying to break through all the excitement and bring some order.

Todd explained that in fact we were writing a book. "A DVD-plus-book sort of thing," he explained, "combining the footage from the interview we did tonight along with this conversation we're having right here."

Rose got quiet. "You mean . . . we might be in your book, Todd?"

"Rose, you're a pastor; you know that every encounter is a potential sermon illustration. So yes, there is a good chance this conversation will make the book."

"Okay, Todd, then this is what I want to know. You are a trained theologian, so you had to have noticed Charlie's comments about Paul usurping Jesus as the tacit leader of Christianity, something people call 'Paulianity.'

Charlie identifies an issue brought up repeatedly by outsiders: Why do we talk so much about Paul and so little about Jesus? **Watch the clip "The Problem of Paulianity."**

And then as if that wasn't enough, he proceeded to school us on how to read the Bible correctly: 'Stick with the red letters—the places where Jesus is speaking directly.' I mean, I liked Charlie, but he's an agnostic, Todd. What were you thinking when he was talking?"

"Here's my take, Rose. I was impressed with Charlie's familiarity with Scripture. Sometimes I think agnostics take the Bible more seriously than believers. But to be honest, comparing Paul and Jesus is an intellectual straw man. It's not fair to pit Paul against Jesus, as if they have counter claims or aims. There have been hundreds of millions of followers of Jesus over the centuries who would say that they owe the vibrancy of their faith in Jesus to Paul's life and writings. Bashing Paul doesn't elevate Jesus. A better tack would be to follow the

Charlie, our atheist guest, talks about his experiences reading the Bible. **Watch the clip "An Outsider's Survey of the Bible."**

teachings of Jesus the way Paul did—and you can bet he was trying to live Jesus's teachings—even if we are struggling with Paul's explanations of what Jesus was thinking and doing."

I know how much Rose and Todd love to discuss theology, but because I had the primary responsibility for getting this book to print, I decided to shift the topic from *orthodoxy* (doctrine) to *orthopraxy* (doing). It took a few minutes, but I was eventually able to get everyone's attention off Paul and back to my favorite person—me.

Insiders Chandra, Matt, and Tony elevate serving above prayer and church attendance. This urge to serve is a growing movement among both insiders and outsiders.
Watch the clip "The Urge to Serve."

"You Seattleites know what I mean when I say nonprofits are a growth industry here. Maybe it's because we're too tolerant in the Northwest. Maybe it's because Bill Gates and Paul Allen live here. Or maybe it's the water (there's plenty of it). Whatever the reason, all of our guests currently work for or expressed interest in working for a nonprofit. It appears that this movement is impacting young people all over the world."

Craig interrupted, "When Audrey said, 'Don't invite me to church—invite me to serve,' I wanted to run from behind the camera and yell, '*Listen to her!*'"

"I agree, Craig," I said. "Audrey nailed it. When I was developing new approaches to evangelism a few years ago, it became apparent to me that Christians were walking right past the easiest opportunity to draw outsiders into their world. Just invite them to serve along with you."

Outsiders want us to include them and invite them to serve alongside us. If Jesus isn't their motive, do we exclude them?
Watch the clip "Spiritual Concierge."

Todd interjected. "I think that's what you mean when you talk about churches becoming the spiritual concierge in their communities. You know how when you walk into the lobby of a really nice hotel and notice that a couple people behind a podium are watching you? They're standing there waiting for you to approach them and ask for help. They're waiting on you to help guide you to what it is that you need. As I see it, when churches become the spiritual concierge for their local communities, that's how they operate."

"Right, and in fact a number of churches are already doing this, but as we can see from Audrey's comments, there's plenty of room for more. But I'll tell you this, Todd: when it comes to image repair in the community, this is the fast track for churches."

That triggered a memory for Todd. "A few weeks ago I was having lunch with the national leader of one of the best-known college campus ministries in America. He told me that almost all the college kids coming to Christ in recent times are coming just the way Audrey suggests: they work alongside Christians who are building a Habitat for Humanity house, or digging wells,

Based on Charlie's criteria, are you a Christian?
Watch the clip "Charlie Describes Christlike."

or feeding the homeless. Along the way some see that there is something real in the Christian community and begin to ask questions about faith in Jesus and what it means to follow him. Think about it, Jim. If you were to do a person-on-the-street interview and ask people if they were Christians, you'd have a far better chance of hearing 'Yes, I believe Jesus died for me' than 'Yes, I'm trying to learn to serve others as Jesus suggested when he washed the feet of the disciples.'"

We were closing in on nine o'clock. I knew we needed to begin to wrap things up.

While Todd and I were engrossed in our conversation about spiritual concierges, Rose and company said their good-byes and were exiting the front door of Third Place Books. I followed along to say good-bye, but mostly I wanted to check out my favorite desserts.

Craig walked over and noticed I was either lost in a big thought or staring at the carrot cake enshrined in the Honey Bear Bakery case. It was the latter. Thankfully he intervened and got me back on track.

"Jim, you really seem to have been impacted by how much this group agreed with each other. What's up with that?"

As we walked back empty handed, I explained my passion for this topic. "As a young believer I was taught to *anticipate* rejection from outsiders. To be brutally honest, I was actually trained to cultivate it. We approached outsiders with a message designed to illustrate just how different we were from 'the world.'" Craig and I sat down with Todd. "We looked for any opportunity to stand up for Jesus, which often meant getting into an argument where we threatened and insulted each other. One of my favorite bumper stickers from that era captured the feeling: 'My God's not dead. Sorry about yours.'

"Since that time the religious right has carried the banner for what I now call the *gospel of difference*. Christians have become known as the people against (fill in the blank). But as I see it this interview revealed how a new kind of Christianity is developing. These young insiders worked just as hard to find ways to connect with outsiders as I had looked for ways to disconnect from them."

Todd noticed we were empty handed.

"Hey Jim, where's my carrot cake?"

"Jesus told me not to buy any for you," I joked.

Todd picked up where I had left off. "Jim, I agree with you about Christians of the previous generation—that's you and me—majoring too often on difference. But here's the challenge we face today. When I've talked to sincere Christians who get what you're saying, they honestly wonder if moving from contrast and difference to conversation and connection won't lead to compromise.

"After all, doesn't the Bible talk about being separate from unbelievers, light not having any fellowship with darkness, and so on? And while the three of us may agree that the church has gotten those texts wrong, those thoughts still sit in the back of people's minds—and it confuses them."

Craig was listening carefully to what Todd was saying. Having grown up in church, he understood the dilemma Todd was referring to, but he still had some questions.

"To be honest," he said, "I've been a little discouraged as we've talked about politics, homosexuality, and abortion. I guess I just don't have much faith that Christians will be able to help narrow those divides anytime in the near future. However, this interview in Seattle has given me fresh hope. It's brought to the forefront something that's been present in all of our interviews: young insiders and outsiders share a commonality in wanting to make the world a better place. I'm going to put my money on people who focus on the things that insiders and outsiders have in common, and *making the world a better place* seems to be at the top of the list. As a bonus, this commonality is incredibly Christlike!"

It was about a quarter to nine. The bluegrass band had left the building and the cleanup people were eyeing our table like crows hopping around road kill.

Todd and Craig were packing up their laptops when I grabbed their attention one last time.

"Hey, before we hit the road I want to tell you a cool story about a church that has remade its image in the community by bringing insiders and outsiders together to bless the community.

"Dan Jacobs is one of the students I coach at George Fox Seminary. He is the associate pastor at a one-hundred-year-old congregation in West Seattle. This is a very conservative church that in the past helped to plant a megachurch and a Bible school. They brought Dan in from the East Coast in an attempt to help them reconnect with their neighborhood and larger community. Like many churches they had become ingrown over time and lost touch with outsiders.

"Dan, who is also an artist, began to meet other artists in the neighborhood and discovered that many of them could not find affordable studio space. He also noticed that his church, West Seattle Christian Church, had an empty school building sitting across the street. He asked the elders if they would be willing to let him rent space out to the local artists in what had once been a thriving Christian school.

"Most of these artists aren't Christians and could create art that might make Christians uncomfortable. But recognizing that they'd been unsuccessful in getting these artists to come to their church for free, the elders decided to let Dan charge them rent, albeit modest. And it worked!

"Today that building is full of both Christian and non-Christian artists, and even better, the church's image in the community has gone from 'fuddy-duddy, withdrawn conservatives' to 'relevant and connected followers of Jesus who like us.' In three short years Dan and his church remade the image of a one-hundred-year-old institution by becoming the spiritual concierge of their community."

"What a great story!" Craig said. "What I like best is that it was a one-hundred-year-old, conservative, anywhere-in-America kind of church. It wasn't young people, emerging church people, or missional people. It was a group of every-day Christians, kind of like my dad, who decided to *do what was doable* for them. It's like they took the five loaves and two fish they had, gave it away to people who weren't in their church, and Jesus did the multiplying."

Todd had stopped packing up his stuff and was taking notes as Craig talked.

"Jim," he said, "in my earlier chapter I talked about how context drives everything, and I realize that we use that ex-planation often in negative ways. But your story about Dan and West Seattle Christian proves context works in a posi-tive way also. Those people had a building and a history in a neighborhood that they used to expand the kingdom of God in a way only they were capable of doing."

Seattle was the final stop on our Outsider Interviews tour. The three of us had met sixteen fascinating people. The churches that hosted us and the people who found our guests had in many cases become our close friends. We had discussed a wide variety of issues, from the power of perceptions to politics to homosexuality. We felt as though we had left no topic unturned in our quest to hear what outsiders *really thought* about the church that claims Jesus as its leader. We did this not because we don't like the church but because we agree with Dietrich Bonhoeffer that "the church is the church only when it exists for others."[2]

I learned so much working with Craig and Todd. Craig is the future. He is cynical at times, but he stays connected. His questions will only serve to help the church become a better place for both insiders and outsiders. Todd truly loves the church. His affection is rooted in gratitude for what he has gained from his long association with followers of Jesus.

Craig and Todd were stuffing their laptops in their bags and finally convinced me to unplug.

SIX LESSONS LEARNED

The Things That Moved Us Most

> The master praised the crooked manager! And why? Be-
> cause he knew how to look after himself. Streetwise people
> are smarter in this regard than law-abiding citizens. They
> are on constant alert, looking for angles, surviving by their
> wits. I want you to be smart in the same way—but for what
> is right.
>
> Luke 16:8–9

If you've ever gone online to search for directions from your
house to your favorite movie theater, you probably used
Google. Once you enter the address in the search bar, Google
provides a standard map view, but they also provide a satel-
lite view—an aerial photo of the location you are looking
for—all from the viewpoint of a bird. Recently, however,
Google added another kind of map called "street view." It
allows you to see the buildings or houses you specifically

want to see, but instead of it being from a bird's eye view, it's from a normal human view—on ground level. It seems that Google remembered something we'd forgotten: given the option, most people will choose pictures over words. We agree with Google that seeing things as they really are, from the street level, is always preferable to a drawing or even a bird's eye view.

Have you ever taken a walk around a neighborhood you normally drive through? You notice all sorts of things you never see when you go whizzing by in the comfort of your air-conditioned car with the music blaring. Sounds, smells, human emotions, and relational drama unfold right before your eyes when you get down on the street.

In this book the three of us decided to park our religious car and get out onto the street to experience the sights, sounds, and feelings of outsiders. We wanted to see things from their point of view. We wanted to hear what outsiders are saying, thinking, and feeling about Christianity in America on the street.

Here's what we learned about them and about ourselves.

Craig

Dialogue Is Easier Than I Thought

I hesitate to talk about my faith. With outsiders, I'm afraid to be associated with the Christian label. With insiders, I'm afraid I'll be judged for the disagreeable aspects of my faith. I think back to a conversation I had last spring with a tableful of conservative Minnesotans. I was at an evangelism conference, and it was my turn to share with the group my experiences with Christianity. For some reason I decided to take a risk and let them see the uncensored me. Much to my surprise, my honesty was reciprocated with curiosity and genuine interest. Under normal conditions I'd first test the waters to see if I thought they could handle it. But this conversation had me wondering if I'd been a little too guarded when talking about topics of faith. Over the course of writing *The Outsider Interviews*, I've tried to be a little more open with people I disagree with, both insiders and outsiders. I've tried to participate in dialogue. And I've found that dialogue is a lot easier than I thought it would be.

In Kansas City, Klarisa and I talked openly about abortion. In Phoenix and Denver, I was able to talk with Elisa and Andrew despite our differences. And in Seattle, I shared colorful dialogue with Audrey and Charlie. I was able to have respectful and insightful conversations about faith with all of them. Throughout this project I've caught myself in conversations about faith with the most random people in the most random places. Something has changed. I feel like a switch has been flipped and I'm now comfortable talking about faith. My Sunday school teachers would be so proud that my light is no longer under a bushel. (Well, they *might* be proud.) My version of "letting my light shine" looks more like an untamed bonfire than a cute flannel board candle. I catch myself being remarkably candid about my Christian upbringing, my doubts in faith, and how I now try to help Christians process why they believe what they believe through my website RecycleYourFaith.com.

I was taught that letting your light shine would be followed by persecution (which meant you were doing a good job). My version of shining doesn't get the same results. People respond by sharing their own experiences with religion and church, and a conversation is started. I used to worry about how people would react to my faith, but now I feel like there's nothing to worry about. I used to try to sell a product called Christianity, but now I just share a little bit of who I am and what I'm excited about; enthusiasm helps.

I'll admit that I've been somewhat intentional in making some shifts in how I interact with people. I've had to de-program some things I was taught and learn some new behavior. With some hesitancy, I'm going to tell you about some of the changes I've made, but you'll have to promise not to think of these things programmatically! Basically it all boils down to me just being myself. Here's what that looks like:

1. I'm trying not to take things so personally when someone disagrees with me. Sometimes people judge me and think less of me based on my beliefs, but more often they just disagree with me.
2. I'm trying to give others permission to believe differently than I do. This is a mindset, not something I verbalize. I've been reminding myself as I get into difficult conversations that it's okay for someone to think differently than I do.
3. I'm trying to speak less in absolutes and more from personal experience. Instead of saying, "Churches are not very relevant," I might say, "In my experience I've found that churches are not very relevant."
4. As others get defensive and debate me, I try to remember that I once was and still can be a debater. Debating is a natural response to difference, and I shouldn't judge others for it. Then I try to respond with dialogue.
5. I'm trying to not jump to conclusions before really getting to know what someone thinks. It's too easy for me to put a label on someone after a few sentences. People are more than labels.
6. I'm trying to ask lots of questions. When I start to get defensive, I try to shift that defensiveness to curiosity.

I am by no means a dialogue expert, but writing this book has taught me that despite incredible differences, dialogue is truly possible—and worth the effort.

Todd

Evangelism Boldness Never Goes Out of Style, but Styles Change

Over the years I've worn several styles of pants—or *trousers*, as our British friends say. I'm not sure any of my pants ever reached the level of *trousers*, but here is how the history of Todd Hunter's pants has unfolded. Junior high school: nothing but Levi's 501s. High school in early the 1970s: I am ashamed to say I wore the occasional big-cuffed, wide bell-bottoms! Young adult life was marked by Dockers cotton pants. In my later professional life I was dressed in middle-of-the-road business slacks. Presently I have an affinity for the comfort of Tommy Bahama loose-hanging silk—when I can afford it!

For the sake of my analogy, *boldness* is like pants: always on, in view at all times, permanently in play. Methods, styles, and approaches to evangelism vary with the requirements of various times and occasions. They should easily move from cotton to microfiber to silk.

But alas, this is easier said than done. We love evangelism so much that suggesting changes is unnerving and unpleasant. Saying that we might change our fundamental approach to evangelism is like proposing we not have Thanksgiving dinner.

But like it or not, we are at just such a crossroads. The two or three generations reading this book need to make big changes to interact well with the outsiders we have been introduced to. The older parents among us need to learn the boldness of listening. Yes—it is bold to speak up, but it is even bolder to shut up and listen, to make yourself vulnerable to the assertions and questions of young outsiders.

The young Christians reading this book need the boldness to speak up. Go back and watch Andrew on the Denver Outsiders Interview. He modeled something very close to what I'm trying to express. He clearly loves Jesus and has devoted his life to helping others encounter Jesus, but he shared that confidence with a boldness wrapped in humility and authenticity, and most of all *he listened*. There is nothing wrong with being confident in your relationship with Jesus. But as Andrew graciously modeled, that does not mean you have to become unkind, arrogant, or a know-it-all. You are a Christian today because someone had courage on your behalf. Someone took the risk to start a conversation. Someone ignored the butterflies in their sick stomach to try to say just the right thing to you.

The boldness to listen, to participate in a conversation about faith—this is evangelism for our times.

Jim

Collaborate or Die

I first saw this slogan about ten years ago. A man dressed in a business suit stood on the steps of a courthouse looking all protest-y, holding a placard-type sign with the words "Collaborate or Die!" high above his head. I thought it was a cool marketing campaign but failed to realize how sociologically prescient it was.

From Kansas City to Seattle we heard insiders and outsiders calling for unity. Where we expected deep difference, we discovered radical acceptance. What many of us call compromise, they call connection. Brand loyalty is on the bubble, but community loyalty has never been stronger.

The version of Christianity both Boomers and Millennials (aka the "Kinnaman cohort") inherited was largely developed and nurtured by type A personalities like Billy Graham, Bill Bright, Bill Hybels, and Rick Warren. It was forged in the consumer culture of Christian America, which is reflected in the way church is done every weekend in over 335,000 locations. Many of the young insiders we met were raised in these churches.

162

While this culture shift has been brewing for several hundred years, the change has become increasingly visible over the past twenty. While Boomers have been on the main stage playing out their final act of influence, the Millennials have been backstage playing video games, waiting for them to exit.

But like Columbus accidentally bumping into the Americas while looking for India, on our way to another conclusion the three of us ran into a wonderful surprise.

In these Outsider Interviews we discovered that Millennials are neither as independent nor as cynical as their Gen X cousins. They actually want input and guidance. Here's a street-view example of what I mean by this.

Audrey, one of our Seattle outsiders, shared a letter with me that she wrote to her boss outlining five things she'd like him to know about how she sees things (if he was interested). The letter was never sent (for reasons that will become apparent), but Audrey's insights and appeals provide *an unvarnished view* of what it will take if we're serious about constructing a bridge between generations:

1. Give me things you expect me to research. Don't assume that any research I might do that exposes different viewpoints from yours (the boss's) is because I'm being insubordinate.
2. Give me feedback all the time. I'm used to instant communication, and if you want me to stay connected to you and this organization, I have to feel like we're in conversation (and hopefully dialogue).
3. Ask me what skills I want to build for my next position—and help me build them. All of us pretending that

I'm going to stay in any job longer than a few years (or maybe even a field for longer than a few years) is silly, and being able to be honest about what I want and why I'm in a given job will help us be more open and honest in general.

4. Ask me about the changes I would make if I was in charge of everything, sincerely listen to my answer, and at least consider implementing a few of the ideas. (Bonus points if you let me help implement them, and double word score if you make it public that it was my idea.) The more opportunities you give me to get out, learn something new, and bring that knowledge back, the longer you'll keep me at this company.

5. Don't let *anyone* make negative comments regarding my age (or lack of experience, etc.). If it wouldn't be kosher to say, "You're decrepit!" it's not kosher to say, "You're a baby!" Don't make me defend myself on this; be the boss (man up!) and take it upon yourself to confront any kind of discrimination immediately. This is maybe the most common form of harassment I've experienced, and I've *never* had a boss stick up for me.

Do you feel the frustration and pain in Audrey's voice when she says, "I've *never* had a boss stick up for me"? People who are competing for the same position have no interest in protecting the person they're vying against. But coaches do. If we want to build a bridge to Millennials, then Boomers like me will have to begin thinking more like coaches and less like players.

Because Audrey is a Millenial, she *assumes* shared power. She knows she will get it sooner or later. She would just prefer to have it handed over graciously rather than wresting it from the death grip of her last Boomer boss.

Electricity results when you connect positive and negative poles. Look around you and name one man-made object you see that has not been touched by electricity. Here's my point: *innovation lies at the intersection of difference.*

From my point of view, Boomers have an activist streak and Millennials an optimistic one. When these differences intersect, a unique force field is created that can facilitate the building of a bridge not only for themselves but for all the outsiders who are trying to find their way into the kingdom. When intergenerational activists and optimists collaborate, innovative practices and unpredictable acts of love emerge.

Craig

Dialogue Is Harder Than I Thought

Before this project started I naïvely thought that with a little bit of effort, my dad and I might be able to have conversations about faith without arguing. A couple months later, I'm not even sure a lot of effort is enough. For the time being we're going to have to just keep trying and hope that we might eventually make some progress. How can dialogue be both easier *and* harder than I thought? I guess it all depends on *who* you're talking to. My dad and I might want to have conversations just as much as the next guy, but there's something about our relationship that makes it nearly impossible no matter how hard we try.

I could continue to process why some people are harder to dialogue with than others, but the fact will still remain: we will always have people in our lives who seem utterly impossible to talk to. In lieu of solving that problem, I thought I'd offer a few things I'm looking for from people I find difficult to talk with:

1. Treat me with some dignity. You may think I am dead wrong, but the more you tell me I'm wrong, the less I'm going to listen to you.
2. Don't try to prove me wrong. If you'd like to share how you've come to believe a certain way, that's great. But I'm going to start tuning you out the second you start referencing absolutes I can't argue with (yes, that means Scripture).
3. When you do talk about Scripture, please keep in mind that I may approach Scripture differently than you do. Don't use Scripture as a weapon.
4. Pay attention when I'm talking, and don't cut me off.
5. Try asking some questions. Genuine interest goes a long way with me.
6. Don't label me or call me names. Don't call me a baby killer when I tell you about loving someone who chose to have an abortion. Don't call me a humanist when I tell you about how I respect other religions.
7. When I ask you a question, be honest with me. Tell me how you really feel, not what you think I need to hear.
8. Let me know you're invested long-term in our relationship. I view my faith as a journey, so I want to know you don't view me as a short-term project.

While there may not be a quick fix for people like my dad and me to have open conversations, I do think (in most cases) it's worth the effort.

Todd

Everything I Learned about Dialogue Since I Knew It All

In the "Phoenix Outsiders" chapter Jim wrote about my not-so-brilliant conversation with Erin and Abdo. He was nice about it onstage—always a professional—and even kind in his retelling. But I know him well enough to know that in the moment he was probably really thinking, *I cannot believe my friend Todd is being so stupid—and on camera!*

But come on . . . someone defend me here. Who would ever think *lost* is such a complicated word? I *lost* my car keys. What's hard to understand about that? Well, nothing, but as I talk about in my chapter "Things Change," everything is understood in a certain context.

Working with Craig and Jim and my new outsider friends, I learned that even though I have taught on evangelistic listening and dialogue all over the country and in several seminaries, there was more I needed to know *since I knew it all*.

I needed a deeper experiential knowledge to augment my intellectual knowledge.

With that in mind, here are a few more details about dialogue that I picked up on while writing this book:

1. My presuppositions always need to be checked. They are not evil or to be ignored. There is no way to do life without hypothesis or working assumptions. Just don't marry them. Get hitched to your conversation partner, checking your presumptions as you go.

2. I'm not as neutral or good as I think—at least I cannot assume I will be experienced that way by outsiders. Self-awareness is the door to dialogue.

3. Outsiders—"they"—are not as close-minded or God-forsaken as I may think. We've heard it so many times that I fear it no longer penetrates our consciousness or that we reject it as New Age, but it is true: the vast majority of outsiders genuinely desire a spiritual life. They would love to talk about it if they could find some good dialogue partners.

4. We need little a less *us* and *them* and a little more *we*. This would get us a long way down the street called dialogue. When we come across as fully knowledgable or having fully arrived at conclusions, we are not very good conversation partners. Craig and our outsider friends seem to know this really well. They are natives. I am migrating there.

5. One final, crucial thought: listening and the capacity for dialogue are first a quality of being, not an evangelistic tactic. Working the classic Christian disciplines in pursuit of spiritual transformation, we must become

169

the kind of persons for whom open-hearted, honest, noncoercive dialogue is natural, normal, and routine.

You know what I think? If Jesus were speaking in public today, maybe he would amend his words to include that it is *out of the abundance of the heart the ear does listen and the mouth does dialogue.*

Jim

The Urge to Serve

Hands down, the single most dominant theme to emerge from our interviewees regardless of location or religion was this: "We want to serve others." We heard it from Rio who is gay, Sam the non-Christian Christian, Alex the Christian pre-med student, Matt the Young Life worker, and Charlie the atheist. Outsiders, insiders—they've all got *the urge to serve*.

I was taught to explain this impulse among outsiders as their effort to "earn heaven." My intention is not to minimize the reality of heaven or the fact that some people may believe they will get there through good works, but a least among the people we talked with, the topic of heaven (or for that matter, fear of hell) almost never came up, including from the Christians.

I don't know what happened to talking about the rapture or end times (some of the key selling points I was taught to utilize in the early days of my Christian experience), but it appears from our work on the street that something has changed. The focus seems to have shifted from *getting hu-*

mans to heaven to *getting heaven to humans.* I was trained to believe that getting people to heaven was job number one. Now the focus among young insiders seems to have shifted to helping make the world a better place.

I realize that this might make older insiders nervous, but here's the good news: even though young Christians want to make the world a better, safer, cleaner, and more just place, this doesn't mean they've abandoned the hope of heaven or stopped wanting their outsider friends to join them there. They've simply found common ground on which to stand with their outsider friends and a way to express their faith that is more practical.

My hunch is that many young insiders who were raised in consumerist Christianity have grown weary hearing about how to make *their* lives more abundant. If current research on Christian marriage is to be believed, at least half of these insiders have watched their parents get divorced or devote the best of their lives to accumulating things on earth while talking about how great it will be to go to heaven someday. This mixed message has caused young insiders to double-check their spiritual goals. Combine that with the growing global awareness, facilitated in no small part by the internet (MySpace, Facebook, and Twitter to be specific), that millions of people are *already suffering a hellish existence* and you begin to understand why insiders are requiring a more practical expression of the gospel. Someone put it this way: young insiders want a little less Billy G. and a little more MLK.

The good news is that outsiders want the same thing. We can't be sure why, but for whatever reason more and more outsiders are devoting themselves to serving others as well. Frankly, from an evangelistic perspective, it's an opportunity the church can't afford to ignore. Outsiders like Audrey in Seattle put it plainly: "Don't invite me to church—invite me to serve." Outsiders are asking us to provide them with opportunities to make their world a better place, to advocate for the poor and powerless. In many ways they are inviting us to become better followers of Jesus.

Instead of *reaching out* to them, we join them to work for the common good. Saint Patrick did the same when he broke tradition and intentionally built his monasteries next to the village instead of far away.[1] We do our ministry work *with* outsiders—we invite them to serve with us and we join their efforts to serve others.

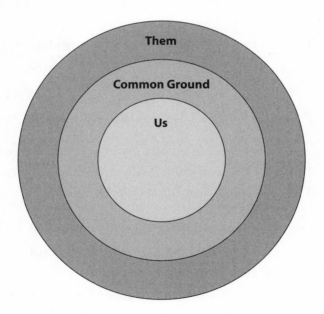

I think this is why Jesus said to his disciples, "I want you to be smart in the same way—but for what is right" (Luke 16:9).

My translation: follow the lead of outsiders, because when it comes to being streetwise, they're smarter than you are. Copy them, emulate them, build relationships with them. You never know—when it's all said and done, they might be the ones waiting for you in heaven.

Coming In for a Landing

Here's a short history of Christianity attributed to Priscilla Shirer. For me, it captures the dilemma and dream for Christianity:

> In first century in Palestine, Christianity was a community of believers.
> Then it moved to Greece and became a philosophy.
> Then it moved to Rome and became an institution.
> Then it moved to Europe and became a culture.
> Then it moved to America and became a business.[2]

There are two kinds of explorers: those who return saying "You should've been there" and those who return *with a map*. We hope this book serves as a map that

> invites you to travel to new places in your spiritual life;
> inspires you to start new relationships with outsiders, insiders, and everyone in between; and
> expands your notion about the true size of God's heart.

APPENDIX

A Reading Guide for Groups and Individuals

The purpose of this guide is to help you continue processing the content of this book either in a group setting or on your own. We hope it helps you grapple with the implications of *The Outsider Interviews* and incorporate what you have learned into your daily life. For each chapter we offer a few introductory statements and then questions and comments to consider. Enjoy.

Chapter 1: The Backstory

Welcome to our story. Be sure to "watch this book." Our journey into the lives of outsiders impacted us on a deep level. We think it will do the same for you.

Questions to Consider

1. Jim talks about the word *lost* and Christians' habit of using it to describe non-Christians behind their backs. Is *lost* part of your religious lexicon? How do you feel about that word? Do you use it in front of "lost" people? Why or why not?
2. Jim says, "Thousands of young Christians are staying under the big tent of Christianity but refusing to toe the party line." What do you think he means by this? Do you agree with him? Why or why not?
3. What do you think we have to learn from outsiders? What do you think Jesus meant when he told his disciples, "The people of this world are more shrewd in dealing with their own kind than are the people of the light" (Luke 16:8 NIV)?
4. Jim compares the impact of the printing press to that of the internet. How has the internet changed or impacted your life? How do you make sense out of the

more disruptive elements of this technology? How do you deal with the speed of new technologies that are being invented every day because of the internet?

5. When it comes to adopting new ideas or practices, some of us are explorers and more of us are travelers. Which category do you fit in? How have you struggled with accepting people who are different from you?

6. Jesus was easy on outsiders and tough on insiders. How have you seen Christians follow or not follow Jesus's example?

7. What do you make of Jim's shorthand for Jesus: "Jesus is the God who *likes* people"?

Chapter 2: Kansas City Outsiders

Being critiqued is tough. It's hard to avoid reacting and defending ourselves. We don't like it when people *compare our worst with their best*. But every now and again it's necessary all the same.

Questions to Consider

1. If you're a Christian, having now heard the critique of some outsiders, how does their critique make you feel? Do you agree or disagree with their perceptions? Explain.
2. The authors suggest that when it comes to understanding the current culture, some people are natives and others are immigrants. Into which category do you fit? What do you think are the implications of this?
3. Watch the clip "The Christian Label." Sarah expresses her resistance to being called a Christian even though she is one. What label or description do you use to explain your faith or beliefs? How do other Christians and/or outsiders respond to this?
4. Watch the clip "Is Love All You Need?" The outsiders boil their understanding of following God down to

"follow the Golden Rule." Would you like to add to this? If so, what would you add? If not, why not?

5. Klarisa speaks transparently about her painful decision to have an abortion and the support her Christian friend provided. Have you ever experienced a moral dilemma and sought the support of Christians? What was the response?

6. The authors talked about the powerful influence "Christian consultants" can have on outsiders. Share about a situation when an outsider invited you to be their Christian consultant.

7. Tell about a time someone listened to you when you really needed it and the impact it had on your life.

Chapter 3: Things Change

Post-Christian. Postmodern. New atheism. Welcome to *your* culture. Church steeples disappear while cell phone towers rise. Not exactly your grandparents' world is it?

Just as Paul leveraged Roman culture to advance the gospel in the first century, Billy Graham used "every modern means" available in the twentieth century. Both men were "anchored to the Rock and geared to the times." Both men navigated their culture, and even exploited it to advance the gospel, without being consumed or controlled by it.

What about us, the twenty-first-century church? Are we willing to follow Paul's challenge to the Corinthian Christians? "I kept my bearings in Christ—but I entered their world and tried *to experience things from their point of view*" (1 Cor. 9:22, emphasis added).

Questions to Consider

1. What is your perception of how Billy Graham influenced modern-day Christianity? Share *your* Billy Graham story if you have one.
2. In this chapter Todd wrote, "Outsiders believe the only things Christians care about is being right and proving others wrong. They believe that in conversations with

Christians there is an undercurrent of arrogance." Perhaps you feel this is overstated; maybe Todd is taking it too far. How would you compare your perception of Christians to the one Todd describes?

3. Todd wrote, "There is no such thing as effective evangelism that is not reflective of its cultural context." What is your favorite form of evangelism? In what cultural context was that methodology most effective?

4. Todd said risk-free ways of doing evangelism do not exist. What kinds of risks have you taken in the past to reach people with the gospel? How have you changed your evangelism methods over time? What are the risks associated with evangelism in your mind?

5. Think of someone you would like to see follow Jesus. How have your "evangelistic attempts" gone with them? If this chapter evoked some new ideas you might apply, what are they?

Chapter 4: Phoenix Outsiders

Christians are called *believers*. Our unique set of beliefs is central to our identity. Outsiders are confused about our beliefs while we're often blinded by them. Do your beliefs blind you?

Questions to Consider

1. What do you find most interesting or surprising about the video clip "Backstage with the Outsiders"?
2. Jim asked Beth to find a Muslim between the ages of nineteen and thirty who would be willing to be interviewed in a church. If someone asked you to take on that task, where would you begin?
3. A Christian audience member challenged the way Jim explained the gospel to the outsiders (accept Christ and you go to heaven; reject Christ and you go to hell). Did this offend you as well? Why or why not?
4. Watch the clip "In or Out? Erin Wants to Know." Erin asks a piercing question: "How much of the Bible do you have to believe to be saved? Sixty percent? Eighty percent?" How would you answer her? What parts of the Bible confuse you?

5. Todd and Craig expressed different points of view about the role of beliefs. Which of them articulated a position you identify with? Why?

6. Watch the clip "Navigating Difference." Alyssa talks about being in relationship with people who don't agree with her Christian views but are still her friends. Could you name those people in your life? How could you go about making friends with more non-Christians?

Chapter 5: The Big Question

Outsiders *flocked* to Jesus, even though he told them the truth. Why do you think they wanted to be with him? Was it something in his eyes, his voice, or his body language?

Questions to Consider

1. Recall a time you were invited to have coffee with someone, thinking it was a gesture of friendship, but it turned out to be a sales pitch. How did you feel about being "baited and switched"?
2. Kirk schedules 25 percent of his time "hanging out" with outsiders. How does his use of church time strike you? What do you suppose Jesus would say about Kirk's practice?
3. Kirk invited outsiders to join his church on a mission trip. Have you ever been part of a group that intentionally included outsiders in the context of serving others? How did it turn out for you and for them?
4. Jim suggests that the most important question to ask outsiders is *not* "If you died right now, do you know for sure you'd go to heaven?" Have you ever participated in an evangelism program that trained you to ask some-

thing unnatural or awkward? What was that experience like for you?

5. Jim suggests that 90 percent of evangelism programs might have to be eliminated if we held them to the test of "loving others the way you want to be loved." Is this too simplistic? How would you modify his statement?

6. Talk about an outsider you *like*, someone you would enjoy spending more time with and learning about.

Chapter 6: Denver Outsiders

Birds of a feather flock together, and so do Christians. *Difference* makes us uncomfortable, afraid, and sometimes angry. Separating ourselves from difference has even become a sign of maturity for Christians. But what if one of *your* friends "goes different" on you? What then? It's happening all around us. It may have already happened to you.

Questions to Consider

1. If you watched the Denver interview with a group, share with each other the feelings it prompted or provoked in you. Try not to correct, fix, or analyze each other's feelings. Just listen. If you're not in a group, simply note what emotions came up for you when you watched this interview.

2. In the clip "Insiders and Gay People," Tony (who is a Christian) says two things: (1) Jesus would have hung out with gay people, but (2) Jesus *would* have had an opinion about their moral choices. How does Tony's view compare with your own view of how Jesus would handle this issue?

187

3. Watch the clip "Damaged by Labels." When have you been labeled? How did it impact you, and how long has the memory of this experience stayed with you?

4. In the clip "Remaining Open," Andrew talks about holding some things with a closed hand and others with an open hand. What issues do you hold with a closed hand, and what issues do you hold with an open hand?

5. Craig asks why homosexuality gets so much more attention than gluttony, cheating, lying, divorce, and adultery. If someone were to ask you this question (maybe someone has!), how would you respond?

6. Todd suggests that if we want to find fish, we are going to have to go where they are. What practical steps would you need to take in order to get closer to where the fish seem to be biting these days?

7. Watch the clip "Rio's in the Middle." How do you respond to the fact that Rio minimizes her sexual identity issues but seems quite concerned that she may not be serving as much as she could?

Chapter 7: Getting Past Gay

We think this might be the most important chapter of the book. We wrote *The Outsider Interviews* in part to help parents understand their kids. Things change. Today's twenty-somethings are different from those of earlier generations. That's why Craig wrote this chapter.

Questions to Consider

1. Craig said, "I started a process I now call 'recycling my faith' where I pressed the reset button and started over. I kept some beliefs and discarded others, but I primarily reshaped the things I'd been taught to better reflect my personal experience with God. I call this recycling because I didn't just discard the faith I grew up with; rather I reused and redeemed parts of it so that it could be useful in my life today. I began to trust myself and Jesus a little more and what I'd been taught a little less." Does Craig's term "recycling faith" work for you? Why or why not? What beliefs have you recycled?
2. Craig said to his father, "But I don't see us coming to any conclusions about that topic. I just want to explore whether it's possible for us to talk about something like homosexuality without it resulting in an anger-filled,

intellectual debate." We have difficulty talking about differences. The categories that most often trigger these kinds of feelings seem to be religion, politics, and sexuality. In what relationships have you been able to talk about these sensitive topics without the relationship falling apart? What is necessary for such an interaction to take place?

3. At one point Craig apologizes to his dad for judging him. Have you ever apologized to your parents or anyone for judging them? How did that experience change you? How did it impact the relationship?

4. Craig's dad expresses frustration with homosexuals who "seem hyper-sure of themselves" and "want to shove their lifestyle in our faces by parading their relationships and complaining about not having equal rights." Gay people, of course, accuse Christians of the very same practices. What do you make of this dynamic? How might Christians engage it constructively?

5. Craig summarizes what he wants from his dad this way: "I just want to feel as though he accepts me even if he disagrees with me." Why do you think this is so important to Craig?

6. This chapter doesn't have a happy ending. That's because Craig and his dad remain in a process. Lack of resolution is frustrating. Are you in a relationship that is to some extent unresolved? If so, what is difficult about this? What gives you hope about your relationship?

Chapter 8: Seattle Outsiders

This chapter addresses two issues: (1) outsiders' and insiders' perception that Christianity is overly-involved in politics, and (2) outsiders' and insiders' desire to serve others.

Questions to Consider

1. In the clip "Republican Christian Oxymoron?" Brian, a Christian from South Africa, takes issue with American Christians being one-issue voters, and Erin, an outsider, says, "I've never met a Christian who isn't a Republican." If Brian and Erin made these observations directly to you, how would you respond?
2. How do you make sense of the reality that while most African American Christians vote Democratic, most white Christians vote Republican? How would (or do) you explain this well-known divide to outsiders?
3. Rose asked Todd about Charlie's comments regarding Paul being given prominence over Jesus in modern-day Christianity (see clip "The Problem of Paulianity"). Does Paul get more "air time" than Jesus in your church? How would you have responded to Charlie's inquiry?
4. In the clip "Spiritual Concierge," Chandra (an insider) and Audrey (an outsider) say essentially the same thing:

serving others is a spiritual activity. Many Christians have been taught that outsiders' only motive for serving others is to earn a ticket to heaven (aka good works). What do you sense is Audrey's motive?

5. The clarity of Audrey's plea, "Don't invite me to church—invite me to serve," is startling to us. In one sentence it captures the value shift we sense taking place among young insiders. In the past, obeying Jesus was interpreted to mean personal morality; now it includes *serving others*. Why do you think this shift is taking place? Does it concern or comfort you?

Chapter 9: Six Lessons Learned

With the interviews in the rearview mirror, the three of us took time to reflect. What was going on in the minds of Todd, Craig, and Jim on a deeper level? What were the things that impacted them the most?

Questions to Consider

DIALOGUE IS EASIER THAN I THOUGHT

"I was at an evangelism conference, and it was my turn to share with the group my experiences with Christianity. For some reason I decided to take a risk and let them see the uncensored me."

Have you, like Craig, shared your real feelings with some Christians, knowing you were taking a risk? If so, what happened?

EVANGELISM BOLDNESS NEVER GOES OUT OF STYLE, BUT STYLES CHANGE

"It is bold to speak up, but it is even bolder to shut up and listen, to make yourself vulnerable to the assertions and questions of young outsiders."

Todd flips the meaning of boldness from preaching to listening. When have you exercised the courage of listening to people say something you really didn't want to hear?

Upon reflection, was it a good decision? How did it impact that relationship?

COLLABORATE OR DIE

"Audrey, one of our Seattle outsiders, shared a letter with me that she wrote to her boss, outlining five things she'd like him to know about how she sees things (if he was interested)."

Review Audrey's list. Which points do you identify with, and which ones seem over the top? Why?

DIALOGUE IS HARDER THAN I THOUGHT

"I could continue to process why some people are harder to dialogue with than others, but the fact will still remain: we will always have people in our lives who seem utterly impossible to talk to. In lieu of solving that problem, I thought I'd offer a few things I'm looking for from people I find difficult to talk with."

Review Craig's list. Which of his points pushes your buttons, and why do they do so?

EVERYTHING I LEARNED ABOUT DIALOGUE SINCE I KNEW IT ALL

"One final, crucial thought: Listening and the capacity for dialogue are first a quality of being, not an evangelistic tactic. Working the classic Christian disciplines in pursuit of spiritual transformation, we must become the kind of persons for whom open-hearted, honest, noncoercive dialogue is natural, normal, and routine."

If, as Todd suggests, evangelism meant the spiritual practice of noncoercive dialogue, how would that change the way you share Jesus with people?

THE URGE TO SERVE

Take a look at the chart "Us/Them/Common Ground." What are the *common ground opportunities* between you and the outsiders in your life? What can you do this week to begin cultivating those opportunities?

NOTES

Chapter 1: The Backstory

1. David Kinnaman and Gabe Lyons, *unChristian: What a New Generation Really Thinks about Christianity . . . and Why It Matters* (Grand Rapids: Baker, 2007).

2. Dietrich Bonhoeffer, *Letters and Papers from Prison*, ed. Eberhard Bethge, trans. Reginald Fuller et al., enlarged ed. (New York: Touchstone, 1997), 382.

3. Peter Drucker, *Post-Capitalist Society* (New York: Harper, 1993), 1.

4. Phyllis Tickle, *The Great Emergence: How Christianity Is Changing and Why* (Grand Rapids: Baker, 2008), 27.

5. Daniel Goleman, *Emotional Intelligence: Why It Can Matter More Than IQ* (New York: Bantam, 1995), 162, emphasis added.

Chapter 3: Things Change

1. Kinnaman and Lyons, *unChristian*, 15, 24, 33.

2. Ibid., 26.

3. Ibid., chaps. 2 and 3.

4. Ibid., 25.

5. Ibid., 29.

6. From everything I know from being around Billy Graham just a little bit, from everything I have read, and from those mutual acquaintances between Graham and myself, I know that Billy would not like attention being drawn to himself in any untoward way. I am quite sure he thinks of himself as just a man, a blessed and gifted servant of the gospel.

7. William Martin, *A Prophet with Honor: The Billy Graham Story* (New York: Harper, 1992), 93.

8. Ibid.

9. John Pollock, *Billy Graham: The Authorized Biography* (New York: McGraw-Hill, 1968), 56.

10. Ibid., 51, 61; Martin, *A Prophet with Honor*, 91.

11. Kinnaman and Lyons, *unChristian*, 71.

12. "Inquirer" was the name given to outsiders before "seeker" became the norm.

13. These ideas come mostly from a November 2006 *Wired* feature article by Gary Wolf titled "The Church of the Non-Believers." See http://www.wired.com/wired/archive/14.11/atheism.html.

14. "In God's Name," *The Economist*, Nov. 1, 2007.

15. See especially chaps. 1–3.

Chapter 4: Phoenix Outsiders

1. See Matthew 7 in *The Message*.

2. From *The Problem of Pain* and *The Great Divorce*, in Wayne Martindale and Jerry Root, eds., *The Quotable Lewis* (Wheaton: Tyndale, 1990).

3. See Matthew 8:10.

Chapter 5: The Big Question

1. See Dan Kimball, *They Like Jesus but Not the Church: Insights from Emerging Generations* (Grand Rapids: Zondervan, 2007), 42–43.

2. See Brian McLaren, *More Ready Than You Realize: The Power of Everyday Conversations* (Grand Rapids: Zondervan, 2002) for the best example of the power of noticing.

Chapter 6: Denver Outsiders

1. See Paul G. Hiebert, *Anthropological Reflections on Missiological Issues* (Grand Rapids: Baker Academic, 1994), chap. 6.

2. For example, see William J. Webb, *Slaves, Women and Homosexuals: Exploring the Hermeneutics of Cultural Analysis* (Downers Grove, IL: InterVarsity, 2001).

Chapter 7: Getting Past Gay

1. "Fifty-eight percent of young white evangelicals support some form of legal recognition of civil unions or marriage for same-sex couples" ("Survey: Young Evangelical Christians and the 2008 Election," *Religion and Ethics Newsweekly*, September 29, 2008, http://www.pbs.org/wnet/religionandethics/week1204/survey.html).

2. See Kimball, *They Like Jesus but Not the Church*, and Bruce Bickel and Stan Jantz, *I'm Fine with God . . . It's Christians I Can't Stand* (Eugene, OR: Harvest House, 2008).

Chapter 8: Seattle Outsiders

1. Melissa Etheridge, "I Need to Wake Up," *Greatest Hits* (New York: Island, 2005).

2. Bonhoeffer, *Letters and Papers from Prison*, 382.

Chapter 9: Six Lessons Learned

1. George G. Hunter III, *The Celtic Way of Evangelism: How Christianity Can Reach the West . . . Again* (Nashville: Abingdon, 2000).

2. Pricilla Shirer quoted at Quotiki, http://www.quotiki.com/quotes/13471.

Jim Henderson is the co-founder of Off The Map, CEO of Jim Henderson Presents, and founder of Church Rater. He has written two books on the topic of connecting with Outsiders: *Evangelism Without Additives* and *Jim and Casper Go to Church*. He holds a Doctor of Ministry degree from Bakke Graduate University. He and his wife Barbara live near Seattle, Washington.

Todd Hunter, bishop for The Anglican Mission in the Americas, is the founding pastor of Holy Trinity Anglican Church in Costa Mesa, California. Author of *Christianity Beyond Belief* and *Giving Church Another Chance*, Todd is also the founding director of Churches for the Sake of Others, the West Coast church planting initiative for The Anglican Mission in the Americas. Todd also founded Three Is Enough, a small-group movement that makes spiritual formation doable. Todd and his wife Debbie live in Eagle, Idaho, with their two children, Jonathan and Carol.

Craig Spinks is the owner of Quadrid Productions, a production company that specializes in capturing real-life stories that challenge, inform, and motivate. He has done work for Billy Graham Mission, Focus on the Family, Henry Cloud, Association of Vineyard Churches, and Vineyard Music. Craig also runs a website called Recycle Your Faith (RecycleYourFaith.com) where each week a compelling spiritual topic is introduced through a short video and a vibrant online conversation ensues between people of different viewpoints. Craig and his wife Sara live in Denver, Colorado.

www.jimhendersonpresents.com